HELLO CANADA!

HELLO CANADA!

The Life and Times of
FOSTER HEWITT

● ● ●

SCOTT YOUNG

SEAL BOOKS
McClelland and Stewart-Bantam Limited
Toronto

HELLO CANADA! THE LIFE AND TIMES OF FOSTER HEWITT
A Seal Book / December 1985

Canadian Cataloguing in Publication Data

Young, Scott, 1918–
  Hello Canada!: the life and times of
Foster Hewitt

Bibliography: p.
Includes index.
ISBN 0-770-42100-8

1. Hewitt, Foster, 1903–1985.   2. Sports-
casters—Canada—Biography.   3. Radio
broadcasting of sports—Canada—History.
4. Television broadcasting of sports—
Canada—History.   5. Hockey—Canada—History.   I. Title.

GV719.H48Y67   1985   070.4'49796962'0924   C85-099538-8

PRINTED IN U.S.A.

COVER PRINTED IN U.S.A.

FG   0 9 8 7 6 5 4 3 2 1

CONTENTS

ACKNOWLEDGMENTS

• • •

IN SOME WAYS I HAVE BEEN RESEARCHING THIS BOOK FOR much of my life, first as a listener to Foster Hewitt's hockey broadcasts and eventually as a broadcast-crew colleague and friend. Yet like many in Foster Hewitt's life, I only knew one part of him. Such breadth and balance as I have been able to present in this book would not have been possible without a tremendous amount of help from those who loved him, worked with him, did business with him, accepted his help and advice, and from some who never had met him.

I owe much to Foster's widow, Joan Hewitt, his son, Bill Hewitt, daughter Wendy Hewitt Rowan and sister Audrey Hewitt, whose keen memory at age eighty-six did much to sketch in the Toronto of Foster's childhood. His colleagues in hockey broadcasting gave generously of their time and memories: H. E. Hough; H. M. Turner, Jr.; Hugh Horler; Bob Gordon; Frank D. Selke; and Nancy Carroll. John Bassett told warmly and colorfully of his association with Foster in establishing CFTO-TV in Toronto and of how Foster's conservative business attitudes helped the station achieve great financial success. Punch Imlach fondly remembered Foster on the road with the Toronto Maple Leafs in some of their great years. Senator Keith Davey's experiences, keen perceptions and anecdotal memories of his time as a salesman at Foster's radio station, CKFH, in its early years, were invaluable.

I also thank King Clancy and Harold Ballard of Maple Leaf Gardens for their help. Fred Dixon of Hewittdale Productions Limited filled in many business and personal details of Foster's last ten years. I am indebted to Joan Taylor and Mary and Gillis Purcell for research assistance, and to Shirley Wilson for her accurate and speedy transcriptions of interview tapes.

Others who helped materially with their knowledge of the subject included Jim Proudfoot and Milt Dunnell of the Toronto *Star,* Dick Beddoes of CHCH-TV, Ted Delaney, vice-president of CFTO-TV, Murray McDonald and Mike Morgan of the CBC and, from their magazine articles, June Callwood, Trent Frayne, Gordon Sinclair, Jack Batten and others. Mary-Anne Mihorean, archivist of the Anglican Church of Canada's Toronto diocese, produced, from an 1875 baptismal record originating in Cobourg, the names of James T. and Sarah Hewitt, who moved to Toronto in 1879 and founded this branch of the family. I am also grateful for the editing skills of Margaret Hogan, Jennifer Glossop and Edna Barker.

In addition, my reading included these invaluable records of Foster and his time: *Down the Stretch* by W. A. Hewitt (Ryerson Press, 1958); *The Leafs: The First Fifty Years,* assembled by Stan Obodiac (McClelland and Stewart, 1976); *Behind the Cheering* by Frank J. Selke with Gordon Green (McClelland and Stewart, 1962); Conn Smythe's memoirs, *If You Can't Beat 'Em in the Alley* (McClelland and Stewart, 1981); and Foster's own books, *Down the Ice* (S.J. Reginald Saunders, 1934); *Hockey Night in Canada* (Ryerson, 1953, revised 1961); and *Foster Hewitt: His Own Story* (Ryerson, 1967).

I should also stress that while I drew freely on all the above sources, my conclusions were my own and any errors or omissions are my responsibility.

Scott Young,
Cavan, Ontario, August 1985.

INTRODUCTION

●●●

DOES THE MAN REALLY NEED AN INTRODUCTION? PERHAPS not now, this minute, when his voice still is heard from time to time in broadcasting retrospectives. But with the proliferation of media stars in the 1980s and onward, and with home sets hooked up to satellite dishes that bring in 150 signals worldwide, perhaps some day the question will be asked: who was Foster Hewitt? The answer is simple enough. He was the first media star in this country and he remained our principal media star for life.

There are two reasons for his longevity in that role. One was that his subject was hockey, precisely as Toscanini's was music. In much the same sense that music is the language of the world, hockey is the language that pervades Canada. The second reason for Foster Hewitt's fame, which lasted through the twilight years when he was much more often in the public mind, or memory, than he was in the public eye, is that nobody could talk the language of hockey as well as he could. Nobody else could bring to it the excitement, the love, the awe. It was a gift.

Once, not long before his death, he was standing in front of an audience that had gathered to see him accept one of his numerous honors and awards. In many minds there was a feeling that it would be nice to know just a little more about why this smallish, unassuming, down-to-earth man had such a hold on the Canadian consciousness.

1

When he explained himself, it was as if nothing really had to be explained except how he got there in the first place, so he did it that way. "Hockey has thrilled and entertained me since I was five years old and my father first started taking me along with him to watch a game," he said. "From that point on it's been a passionate love affair that has lasted most of this century. It's hard to explain why it means so much to me; it's simply that to me hockey has always been the epitome *of everything*."

Courage, resoluteness, recklessness, speed, skill, stupidity, brutality, cupidity, the meek and the bully, the spirit that transcends the skill, beauty and the beast, noise, happiness, regret—those were part of his "everything." It was what he saw and described, never really knowing how he did it except to relate it to a phrase like "passionate love affair."

He was a famous person in Canada, because of radio, when he was twenty-four years old. He died at eighty-two, having simply kept on earning greater and greater fame. He was forty years and more into his career, and still rising toward his peak, before the offical handers-out of awards ("gongs," as the slang has it) realized that he was worth their attention. After that, it was a landslide: the Order of Canada (officer division), the Hockey Hall of Fame, Sports Hall of Fame, gongs in New York, Toronto and Montreal. In Edmonton an honorary degree was waiting but his final illness intervened. One award read: "To the man who made Hockey Night in Canada' a national institution and with his unique and outstanding contribution to the game taught Canadians from coast to coast to know better, and enjoy more."

It was typical, though, of the almost shy surprise with which he always acknowledged his fame that the recognitions he valued most were the relatively simple kind. He had gone every year to the Canadian National Exhibition in Toronto, riding the rides and eating the pink cotton candy. Every year, as he got older, he'd find a day to wander the midway and look at the exhibits. In 1980 they asked him to open the show. As royalty had, and field marshals, and movie stars. Not bad, he laughed, not bad.

It was partly this, the simplicity, added to the passion and love and sheer understanding that he loaded into his communications with Canadian radio audiences, that made him what he was. Sometimes one-third of the nation listened to him, six million people back when we had eighteen million. Sometimes ninety thousand people a year wrote to him. Why? That is part of what this biography attempts to explain.

One major disappointment of his life was that the famous gondola from which he broadcast was trashed during one summer's renovations at Maple Leaf Gardens. It should have been in the Hockey Hall of Fame, he thought, and when he discussed it with one friend he had tears in his eyes. He thought it represented an era, a long era, his era, and it did.

But the day he died something else happened that would have made him laugh. As the quintessential *Anglo* in all of hockey, his rarely jolly interchanges with his French-speaking counterparts in hockey broadcasting were legendary among broadcast crew members.

He died at five forty-five on an afternoon when his longtime Francophone sparring partners were getting ready for a playoff game at the Montreal Forum, the Leafs long since dead and gone for the season.

When the word reached the Forum that Foster Hewitt was dead, the planned opening ceremonies were scrapped. Instead, the announcement was made and the crowd at the Forum stood for a minute's silence in his honor. For that minute of mourning French and English didn't count. That silence showed not only hockey's respect, but also Canada's, for the man who had done more than any other individual to make hockey a sort of Canadian chromosome, possessed by us all.

1
THE BLOODLINES

● ● ●

"With such a rich heredity and in the midst of such a healthy environment, it would seem I was destined almost from infancy for a career with overtones of sport."
—Foster Hewitt in 1953 at a testimonial dinner for his father

IN THE LATE 1870s, WHAT IS NOW DOWNTOWN TORONTO WAS a place of mostly unpaved streets and lanes. Low buildings, horses and stables were everywhere, and the general appearance was one we would associate with that of an overgrown village today. It was to this setting that a family named Hewitt moved. They came from Cobourg, a town on Lake Ontario a few dozen miles to the east. James T. Hewitt, until then a salesman, had been attracted to Toronto by a ten-dollar-a-week job as an inspector of horse-drawn streetcars. Little is known of his early years except that he was born in Canada. His wife, Sarah, was from Northern Ireland and had been a school teacher at Innisville, near Ottawa, before they married.

Over the next few years, the Hewitts, with their four sons, Art, Jim, Fred and Billy, and their daughter, Lilian, lived in at least two rented houses, both of them in what is now the heart of Toronto's downtown. They seem to have been a fairly average working family, except perhaps for the mother's scholarly bent.

Their fourth child was four years old when they moved to Toronto. He was William Abraham Hewitt, called Billy. The Hebraic middle name apparently embarrassed him in the bigoted Toronto of his time. He kept it secret most of his life and appears in some documents as William Arthur Hewitt. Sarah named him for a noted educator, Abraham Code.

In 1883, when Billy was eight, the family suffered a disaster: James Hewitt died. He had been able to provide quite well for his wife and children on his ten dollars a week, but his death left them almost totally without resources. They were forced to move to cheaper quarters in the downtown area. Billy Hewitt remembered later that one of his evening pastimes was to follow the city lamplighter on his rounds, watching him poke his lighted pole into the new streetlights of the time to get them going each dusk. At the time even Bloor Street was considered the outer reaches.

The family scraped by on what Sarah Hewitt could earn from some part-time teaching and the youngsters' odd jobs. One of Billy Hewitt's first jobs was delivering newspapers. He would rise at 3:30 A.M. and pull his wagon or, in winter, his sleigh, down to the office of the *Empire* newspaper, which was then in the downtown Manning Arcade. There he would pick up his papers, ranging from four to eight pages per issue, and deliver them to homes in a large area running north from Queen Street to Carlton Street, and east from Jarvis Street to Sherbourne Street.

Over the ensuing years he had a variety of jobs, sometimes holding two at a time. He polished, graded and packed apples for two dollars a week. He was a messenger in a law office, delivering legal papers throughout the city and between trips copying letters in longhand. (He never learned to type, even when he became one of the best-known newspapermen in the country.) He worked one summer in a factory that made funeral caskets. At age ten, ranging through the city the way a boy will, he even pitched batting practice for the city's professional baseball team.

But, at thirteen, he found a job that was to change his life: the Toronto *News,* at 106 Yonge Street, hired him to hold the written copy while the proofreader checked it against the printed version. Young Billy Hewitt was bold. He also began to write little snippets of news that he would happen across, and some of them were printed. He was attending Jarvis Collegiate at the time. One afternoon after school when he was fifteen years old, he was holding copy for the proofreader when one of the paper's executives came into the room and barked at him, "Is your name Hewitt?"

Billy Hewitt said yes.

"Do you want to be a reporter?"

"Yes, sir." It was the ambition of his life.

"Stand up."

Billy Hewitt stood up. He was five feet seven, weighed about a hundred pounds and wore short pants like all schoolboys of his time. But he passed inspection.

"You're hired. Go home and tell your mother to buy you a pair of long pants and be back here at seven in the morning. Report to the city editor. Your pay will be ten dollars a week."

That day he quit school and bought his first longs. He hardly slept all night. At seven the next morning he was standing in front of the city editor who looked at him, sighed and said, "Go down to the Central Prison on Strachan Avenue and tell the warden you're there to do a story on the strapping."

The prisoner who was to be strapped had been convicted of a sex offense. The warden also sighed when he saw whom the *News* had sent. "Damn shame for the *News* to send a child to such a scene," he grumbled. "But go on in."

Scared stiff, Billy watched a big guard applying a crackling cat-o'-nine-tails to the bent bare back of the prisoner while another guard rubbed on a lotion to inhibit bleeding. He wrote the story in longhand and took it back to the *News* office. That same day he was sent to cover a wedding, then a funeral, then to an insurance company to do a story on whether it intended to pay the policy for a man who had committed suicide. At six o'clock he was finished, and he walked home happy.

At age fifteen, he naturally had no thought that he had embarked on a career that was to be his life. He was named sports editor of the *News* at age twenty, and his salary of twenty dollars a week made him one of the better-paid journalists in the city.

Two years later, after a courtship that began and flourished in the choir at Holy Trinity Anglican Church where they both sang, he married Flora Morrison Foster, whose surname five years later was given to their first son, the most famous Canadian of his time, Foster Hewitt.

There is no doubt that the influences of both parents were essential to what Foster Hewitt became. As far as may be judged from family memories and photo albums, Flora Hewitt was a jolly woman who laughed a lot. Photos show her as stoutish and comfortable-looking, in high-heeled shoes that made her seem a little taller than her husband. Foster and his older sister, Audrey, later remembered her kindliness and understanding and the sheer comfort of being in her company. This might have stemmed partly from her background, which was much more secure than that of her husband. Her father had been a well-off hardware merchant, and her grandfather, with whom she lived after her father's death, which happened before Billy Hewitt met her, was also a successful businessman.

Her grandfather was a man with very strong religious ties and he did not particularly favor Billy Hewitt's associations with prizefighters and horse-racing men. "But," as Billy Hewitt once remarked on this subject, "at least I was an Anglican who not only attended church regularly but also sang in the choir."

To the journalist's catch-as-catch-can life, Flora brought a solidity of purpose and serenity of outlook that helped to shape the life of her daughter Audrey, born in 1898, and the son she bore in 1902 and named Foster.

The other major influence on Foster was Billy Hewitt, who like most journalists was a scrambler in his early days. Boxing was one of his favorite sports, as it had been from the days when the four Hewitt brothers staged fights in their cellar when their mother wasn't home. Soon Art and Jim progressed to fighting secretly for money on fight cards around the city. Billy Hewitt often either worked his brothers' corners or watched as part of the crowd. Jim was a bantamweight and Art a flyweight. Eventually their mother decided that all those bruises and black eyes couldn't be coming from walking into poles by mistake and the secret was out. Both brothers eventually became Canadian champions in their classes.

That boxing tradition and the interest in sports persisted in the family for generations. At one time three of the brothers, the father and two uncles of the then infant Foster Hewitt were sports editors: Fred on the New Orleans *Item* and later with Hearst papers in Chicago and San Francisco, Billy by then (after a change of employers) with the Toronto *Star* and Jim with the Winnipeg *Tribune* and Vancouver *Sun* before he was killed at Passchendaele in 1917 during the First World War.

With that in his background, Foster Hewitt became a boxer, too, first in high school and later at the University of Toronto. When Foster's own son, Bill, was a boy, and Foster, by then famous, was older than forty, the two of them often put on the gloves, shoved some furniture out of the way and had at each other. Bill's memories (forty years later) of those father-son bouts includes this: "Once I got a little overconfident with Dad and the next thing I knew I was flat on my back. He still knew how to hit."

When Foster was a baby, the family home was a three-story semidetached house of solid red brick with a wide veranda at 592 Bathurst Street, on the west side above College Street. His sister, Audrey, remembers that when she was about seven and Foster about three, she used to push him in a baby carriage if they were going someplace too far for him to walk. Once when he was being a particular pest, as small boys sometimes are, she told him if he didn't smarten up she would push him under a Bathurst streetcar. Foster apparently took this threat to heart. Shortly thereafter, out by himself, he fired a rock at a passing streetcar accurately enough that it broke a window. Chased by the streetcar conductor and some passengers, Foster then made what Audrey considered to be a major mistake: "He ran straight home, pursued by this posse, and naturally right into the arms of our mother. That was one of the few times I can remember him being in real trouble around the house."

After a few years the Bathurst Street house was sold and the family moved to 2 Roxborough Street East, at the corner of Yonge Street. The house was sold many years later and a five-story office building stands there now. But for Foster's growing-up years, that house was home base, and it was from there that he was introduced to sports from the inside.

In those days, and indeed for many decades thereafter, it was common for sports editors to make a little extra cash by working in the sports they wrote about. When Foster was a boy, his father, sports editor of the *Star*, was also manager of the Toronto Rugby Football Club, secretary of the Ontario Hockey Association (a post he held for more than fifty years) and publicity man for the Grand Opera House at 11 Adelaide Street West, as well as being involved in everything that came along in the sports world.

Naturally, W.A. Hewitt's cronies were sports people not only in Toronto but elsewhere: his close acquaintances included boxers Jim Corbett, Bob Fitzsimmons, Jack Johnson, Jim Jeffries and baseball's Ed Barrow, later a famous major-league manager with the Boston Red Sox and the New York Yankees. Willie Keeler, one of the most celebrated baseball hitters of the time ("What I do is hit 'em where they ain't"), played in Toronto when the ballpark was on Hanlan's Point, on Toronto Island. Because of his father's profession, Foster often spent time at batting practices and games, and knew many of the players.

It was W.A. Hewitt's frequent habit when covering hockey or other sports to take his children with him. Frequently they would watch a game from their father's side in the press box. Foster and Audrey were along when their father and three Toronto cronies traveled to New York and on to the Yale-Harvard football game at New

9

Haven. Foster must have been very young, because he caused much merriment in the group by insisting to the hotel waiter at breakfast that he wanted "coached" eggs.

In other ways, Foster's childhood was one that many children might envy, spent as it was watching pro baseball from choice seats and shaking hands with celebrated fighters, scullers, lacrosse players and jockeys. Since these things cannot be done without parents willing to take the trouble, there can be little doubt that the warm family bonding brought a sense of security.

Foster's dad apparently would go to any lengths for his family. For five months, from 1 May to 30 September, the family rented a cottage at Hanlan's Point on Toronto Island, where young Foster caught frogs and fished. Only a couple of minutes' walk away was the stadium where he watched International League baseball, fights, track-and-field championships and ate peanuts and drank lemonade. It was idyllic for a boy who loved sports. The big ferryboats disgorging their passengers, the sailboats on the bay, home runs that went right over the roller coaster at the adjoining amusement park: those were the days. Once Foster saw what he recalled judiciously as "quite a good fistfight at home plate between the umpire and Jack Dunn, Baltimore's explosive manager." When Foster was nine, he was one of twenty-two thousand fans for a 24 May baseball game between the Toronto and Providence teams.

When he happened to be in the city and had to get back to the island on a day when the ferryboats were jammed (not only for baseball but for such events as wrestling on horseback, match races involving the great sculler Eddie Durnan, even dog races), he never had to wait in line. The ferry owner, Lol Solman, was a personal friend of his father's. "Because of that I could use the special gate reserved for dignitaries and players."

Solman's motives may not have been entirely altruistic. Solman owned the Tecumseh Lacrosse Club, which played in the Hanlan's Point stadium when the ballteam was away. In those days, as now, it never hurt a sports promoter to do a favor for a sports editor. Foster knew none of that; he only knew that when the lacrosse teams were playing he could run over before the game carrying his own lacrosse stick and throw a few balls with such greats of the time as Charlie Querrie and Fred Rowntree.

One year when the big Eaton Games, sponsored by Eaton's department store, were scheduled for Hanlan's Point, Foster had scarlet fever. Being quarantined, he was confined to the third-floor attic room of the Roxborough Street house while most of the family was at the island home. The worst part for Foster was that the Eatons were importing from the New York Hippodrome none other than the world-famous clown Marcelline. Foster pleaded for the right to go to the games, even if it started a scarlet-fever epidemic. He wailed and implored, but to no avail.

A day before the big event, however, W.A. mentioned Foster's acute disappointment to one of Eaton's directors. The next afternoon someone called up the stairs to Foster's attic isolation ward, "Foster! Go and look from the window on the Yonge Street side!"

Foster looked. There, far below, on the west side of Yonge Street, a crowd was gathering quickly around an open car in which stood . . . it couldn't be! It was!

"Marcelline!" Foster croaked happily.

When the clown saw Foster's head at the open window, he performed what Foster remembered as a lovely, funny show, enjoyed by all those crowding around on the street but directed at just one sick little boy.

2
GROWING UP
● ● ●

"At the time, Babe Ruth was a lanky nineteen-
year-old pitcher with the International League
Providence Grays."
— from a City of Toronto document

IF FOSTER'S BOYHOOD SOUNDS LIKE THE KIND THAT MIGHT
have spoiled a child, there was another side: a considerable dose of self-reliance frequently came hand in hand
with the fun times. For instance, at the age of five, Foster
was sent to a private school on Gerrard Street East, near
Yonge, called the Model School. Audrey also went there.
For both, it was intended as preparation for a step up five
or six years on—Audrey to Bishop Strachan school for
girls and Foster to Upper Canada College prep school.
Still, for a short and slender five-year-old, the Model School
was a pretty big deal.

To get to school, Foster and Audrey usually walked
south from Roxborough Street, then considered to be practically out in the sticks. Then after school they'd walk
home.

In spring, when the family moved to Hanlan's Point,
things were different, especially when Foster first started
school. Kindergarten and Grade One got out at noon, so for
May, June and September of those two school years he was

12

on his own from twelve o'clock on. His father was then working down at the old *Star* building at 20 King Street West. At noon Foster would be picked up by his father or his father's emissary and taken to lunch at Jim McCaffrey's Bay Tree Hotel at 121 Bay Street (a site now under acres of railroad tracks).

McCaffrey, who was also president of the baseball club, was a friend and business associate of W.A.'s. Many of the ballplayers lived at the hotel and were around on afternoons off from what was then strictly daytime baseball. These lunches with promoters, athletes and others of the city's sports fraternity were Foster's earliest entries into the sports world. His favorite sports star at the time was Billy Kelly, the Toronto club manager. "I always identified with him because I was always organizing something and trying to be the big shot," Foster once explained. "He was a good model for that kind of thing."

After lunch there were still hours to wait before he could head for Hanlan's Point with his father. Some days he would be taken to Shea's Theatre at 91 Yonge Street. Shea's was run by two more of his father's buddies, Jerry Shea and Walter Braden. They would put the little guy in a good seat where he could watch the best of the world's vaudeville. Sometimes he'd see the same show five times in one week. Writing more than fifty years later in a book called *Foster Hewitt: His Own Story,* he recalled: "I saw some of the acts so often that I knew the jokes and the routines almost as well as the performers." At Shea's, he saw Charlie Chaplin for the first time.

On Wednesdays there would be a special treat. Instead of going to Shea's, he would be taken along King Street to the Royal Alexandra Theatre's midweek matinee. Who managed the Royal Alex? None other than Lol Solman, his friend of the ferryboats and the Tecumseh Lacrosse Club. Solman would put Foster in a good seat, and he'd be there until his father showed up and took him across the bay to the Hanlan's Point house.

As he advanced in school, of course, his theater-going diminished because he didn't get out of class until midafternoon. By then he was interested in school sports. He had some success in sprints on field days, possibly because there was too little of him to cause any substantial wind resistance. But he preferred team sports like baseball and football. His father had been a good quarterback in senior football, and he later refereed games and managed the Toronto Argonauts. Foster's Model School classmates, figuring some of this know-how must have rubbed off, made Foster the school's football captain. The Model School's playing field was of rolled cinders, which gave the players an extra motivation to avoid being tackled. They also used to arrange as often as possible to play their games away from home on the thick green turf of St. Andrew's College and Upper Canada College.

Foster wasn't bad at baseball either. The school's baseball diamond had been laid out far enough away from the buildings that nobody could hit the ball hard enough to break any of the windows. Nevertheless, once when the bases were loaded Foster hit a home run that sailed far and high, breaking a window in the main building. He ran the bases fearing that he was in for it. But he wasn't: the headmaster, measuring the homer, opined with a smile that the school would replace the window, and Foster was able to bask somewhat as he told the story that night at the family dinner table.

In other ways, too, he followed in his father's footsteps. He didn't deliver morning papers, as W.A. had, or make caskets or polish apples for shipment. In him, the family sense of enterprise took an unusual turn. At the time, and for many years thereafter, one of the finest grocery stores in the country was Michie's on the south side of King Street a few doors west of Yonge Street. Michie's dated back well into the last century, almost to the time when Timothy Eaton opened his first department store a few blocks to the north. Michie's was like a much smaller version of the storied Harrod's in London; you could get almost anything there. Including worms. Which is where Foster Hewitt, age eleven, came in.

He found that Michie's would buy worms for thirty cents a hundred. Foster began to gather and sell them. Even though he had to deliver 110 worms to be paid for

14

a hundred, on somewhat the same principle as bakers applied in those days—that a baker's dozen actually numbered thirteen—Foster's worm business prospered. Someone told him that worms were attracted to mustard. So he would spread the back lawn at Roxborough liberally with mustard. Each night he would wait until dark, then go out with a lantern and gather worms. To keep them fresh for delivery, he would put the worms on damp moss in the bottom of a cardboard box. This led eventually to the first, and perhaps only, business disaster of his career. And it left him so shaken that he gave up the business and never collected another worm, except for his own use.

It happened on a Saturday morning, his main delivery day for weekend fishermen. He boarded a southbound streetcar across from his home and headed downtown for Michie's. Just before the streetcar reached King Street, Foster, holding the box of worms and rising from his seat to head for the back exit, felt a disturbing slithering. He had been too liberal with water when dampening the moss. The bottom had fallen out of his box. As he frantically tried to stem the tide, his whole shipment dropped to the floor. Nearly eight hundred worms, once the realization hit them that they were free, began sloping off in all directions.

First Foster tried to recapture them. When he found he wasn't getting anywhere he decided to take the wise way out, ignore the worms and just get off the streetcar. But the conductor in the middle of the car had seen it all.

"Hey, there!" he called.

Foster halted.

"Get rid of those worms!"

By this time the other passengers were killing themselves laughing or staring in disapproval or looking as if they were about to throw up.

Foster got down on his knees and tried to scoop worms into his ruined container. It was hopeless. The conductor banged his bell impatiently. Foster gave up. Using the sides of his shoes, he kicked and scraped and slushed the worms out onto the pavement. When the last one hit the road, he threw the soggy cardboard after it and began

15

walking back up Yonge Street. A gross income of $2.10 down the drain. He headed home to the company of more dependable beasts, his rabbits.

That year, 1913, besides giving up the worm business, he graduated from Model School and moved to Upper Canada College prep school. He no longer walked to school: he was given his first bicycle and would ride west on Roxborough to Avenue Road, walk his bike up the steep hill past De La Salle College, where some of his Roman Catholic friends went, remount and ride the rest of the way through the big gates to Upper Canada College.

His years at the school were one of the best times of his life. He wrote once, "I tried to absorb the wisdom of the masters; and while I usually squeezed through examinations there were few indications that a noted scholar was on his way." Actually, the indications were a lot more pointed than that. Years later, his youngest daughter Wendy happened upon one of Foster's old report cards in which he was admonished rather forcibly to the effect that if he didn't shape up scholastically he soon would be going to school elsewhere.

Toronto in those days lived up to its sobriquet, Toronto the Good. Sundays were observed so strictly that even the streetcars didn't operate. But the Hewitts beat the rap. It's uncertain now when W.A. bought his first car; in some accounts it was a Model T Ford, but Foster's earliest sharp recollection was of an enormous 1912 Pullman touring car, with polished brass gas headlights and a hand crank. Each Sunday the Hewitts would load up a picnic basket and, with W.A. and Flora in the front, Foster and Audrey in the back, head out for distant climes like Oakville or even Hamilton. Even such short distances could provide adventure in those days. The roads were mostly clay, which turned into clinging mud when it rained.

At Upper Canada College, Foster was introduced to what was to become his best sport, boxing. When he started, he weighed only 103 pounds but, tutored by the school's able physical-training instructor, A.L. Cochrane, his speed and cunning in the ring developed rapidly. He was never beaten in interschool bouts, and he credited Cochrane's influence (they became friends for life) for his winning the 112-pound and 118-pound championships at the University of Toronto and in intercollegiate competition as well, from which he retired undefeated.

A couple of other memorable events took place in Foster's last year at Upper Canada College. Around the Labor Day weekend in 1918, but ten weeks before the end of the First World War, Foster and his mother, father and sister Audrey were heading for a drive through New York State into New England. That year the United States government had ordered all baseball clubs to wind up by Labor Day or else all players would be subject to the nation's "work-or-fight" edict. An extra fifteen days were allowed for the Boston Red Sox and the Chicago Cubs to play the World Series. The Hewitts hadn't aimed specifically at the World Series, but they happened to arrive in Boston on the eve of the Series opener. At the Copley Plaza Hotel they encountered Ed Barrow, who had been a close friend of W.A.'s while Barrow managed the Toronto team to a pennant in 1902. He had just led the Red Sox to the American League championship. Barrow gave the Hewitts an ebullient welcome, offering to leave four tickets for the next day's game.

As it turned out, the tickets were not there as promised the following day. The threat of a strike by the players (which didn't materialize) caused some ugly scenes outside Fenway Park, whereupon the two female Hewitts decided to go shopping. Foster wound up in the press box with his father.

It was a memorable game. The Boston pitcher was Babe Ruth. Four years earlier Foster had seen the Babe, then only nineteen, pitch a one-hitter and hit a home run into Lake Ontario as Providence whipped Toronto 9–0 in an International League game. By 1918 Ruth was beginning to build the reputation that eventually earned him the title "the Sultan of Swat," leading Barrow to take him off the mound so he could play every day. But, said Foster, "for me on that September afternoon in 1918 he was the world's best pitcher." His lefthanded delivery

17

shut out Chicago 1–0 that day. For the next day's game, the Barrow tickets did come through, four in a good box, but Foster always remembered that 1–0 game as the best he'd ever seen.

When the family left Boston, the first tentative reports of a worldwide influenza epidemic were being published. Foster and his father and sister seemed to have light touches of it, but they recovered quickly and the family went on to Atlantic City and Philadelphia. As they headed for home, Flora Hewitt became seriously ill. The family stayed over in Binghamton, New York, for a few days. Flora seemed to recover there, but back in Toronto she had a relapse. For a week or two she was near death. It was three months, around Christmas, before she was allowed out of bed, and for the first six months of 1919 she was able to move around the house only with the aid of crutches.

The epidemic struck one in six Canadians; more than twenty thousand died. Although in time Foster's mother regained her good health, the scare was never forgotten. In 1967 Foster wrote: "Even now, nearly half a century later, when World Series time arrives I still associate what should be a happy sporting time with Mother's almost fatal illness."

3
RADIO TAKES OVER

● ● ●

"When I was growing up, I always believed
that I would go into the newspaper business,
but I didn't want to go into sports because of
my dad. I wanted to make it on my own. When
I was fifteen I started reading and hearing
about a new industry called radio. In those
days nobody knew what radio could mean. But
it all seemed very intriguing to me, especially
after I heard a broadcast of a Jack Dempsey
title fight. That's when I got hooked on the
idea of a career in radio."
                              —Foster Hewitt in 1981

DURING THE FIRST WORLD WAR, RADIO PROVED ITSELF DUR-
ing land battles and in marine communications, but it
remained under strict government control in Britain and
the United States. But if anyone at the time saw radio as
an entertainment medium the idea didn't make headlines.
Its role was entirely official. Radio as a news or public-
service medium was completely unknown, despite its long-
distance capabilities.

With war's end, the government wraps came off
quickly. Radio, which had been developing slowly for nearly
fifty years, suddenly became a hot item. Companies that

had been making radio equipment for military and naval use began casting around for civilian markets to conquer. Among these companies, one of the most enterprising was the fledgling Radio Corporation of America. In 1921 RCA was looking for an event that, when broadcast, would make a public splash and start a rush to buy home radios.

The company found it. That summer Jack Dempsey was to defend his world heavyweight championship against French challenger and European champion, Georges Carpentier. A few radio stations in the United States had been covering small areas with scratchy music, but what RCA had in mind for the 2 July fight in a field outside Jersey City was broadcasting on a hitherto unknown scale.

In late June, not everyone knew just what those "radio" guys were up to, carrying wires and strange-looking devices called microphones around the huge wooden-fenced outdoor arena, but the radio guys were to be a historic part of the fight, which in itself was the biggest event in the first year of what became known as the golden age of sport.

RCA booked about two hundred theaters, some as far away as Florida, and sold tickets with the pitch that the audience would hear a blow-by-blow account of the fight. There were headaches and hang-ups. The equipment was rudimentary, and government intervention in the broadcast was averted only by Franklin D. Roosevelt, then assistant secretary of the Navy.

But when the fighters entered the ring on that blazing-hot afternoon, the setup for the first great radio broadcast of the time was as ready as it would ever be. When Dempsey won in the fourth round, the cheering and wailing spanned half the country before a single newspaper headline had been printed. An era had begun. Never again would a major sporting event go on without those voices, and later pictures, sending each moment around the world.

As Foster noted sixty years later, that single event changed his life as well. Until then, he'd thought that when he finished his arts course at university, which he started in 1918, he probably would look for a job as a newspaper reporter. After the fight, when he thought about his future it was radio he thought about.

Before radio could create its first instant celebrities, Foster Hewitt being one of them, it had to grow up, move from the gadget stage to that of a force in everyday life. Oddly enough, even after the fight broadcast's details were confirmed by newsreel films, many people still refused to believe. During public presentations of the new device there were still some prospective customers who would lift the horn-type radio speakers to see if there was a ventriloquist under the table. The skeptical also included those who didn't believe that anything connected with prize-fighting could possibly be on the up-and-up.

Despite the public incredulity, someone in authority at the Toronto *Star* believed. Who did so is not known now, but he convinced the *Star*'s legendary owner, Joe Atkinson, that if radio was to be the communications medium of the future they'd better check it out.

W.A. Hewitt, as a senior executive at the paper, knew about Atkinson's interest. One day at the dinner table he said to Foster, "There's a big radio show next week in Detroit, open to the public. I'd like to go down and have a look."

Foster, with the enthusiasm that later made his voice the best-known in the land, said, "Gee, so would I, Dad!"

W.A. suggested that Foster talk it over with his mother. It would mean cutting some classes at university. "If she approves, we'll go."

They went.

That trip gave Foster Hewitt his first close look at radio. The fight he'd heard was one thing but he knew little about the technical aspect of how it had been transmitted. Aggressive marketers at RCA were following up the fight broadcast with public demonstrations like the one in Detroit. Among the many curious, W.A. and Foster were directed to a hotel ballroom. W.A., in his memoirs entitled *Down the Stretch,* recalled, "At first the visitors were doubting Thomases. In 1921 people just didn't believe that sounds and voices could be transmitted through walls, across cities, over mountains and be picked up instantaneously at great distances."

In the display were radios and radio parts of many shapes and sizes. One that Foster remembered particularly as a wave of the future was a ten-tube set owned by Henry Ford. It was billed as "the world's greatest radio." The RCA people said that without doubt such sets would be within the financial reach of every American.

The promotional centerpiece was a receiver about twenty feet in diameter. Every half-hour a well-known person would broadcast from a site announced beforehand (so that it could be checked by nosy newspapermen against possible fakery). The doubters would put on the earphones and their looks of scorn would slowly dissolve as they heard some familiar voice identify itself, tell where its owner was at that moment, announce the time and maybe talk a little politics, business or whatever.

In time it was Foster's turn at the earphones. A voice said, "This is Ty Cobb, speaking from Navin Field. The time is now eleven-thirty." And then he went on to talk baseball.

Foster was rarely demonstrative, then or later, but there in Detroit, his father said, "Foster was so enthusiastic about getting into radio that he didn't know what to do first." As it turned out, what he did first was hunt around the hotel for a line of radios he could import to Canada. After checking several brands, he picked one called the Tecla, of the type called crystal sets. These were equipped with an earphone but no speaker. Tuning in something, anything, required carefully moving a wire "cat's whisker" over a tiny chunk of crystal (it looked like a bit of stone) until voices, or music, or whatever, could be heard above the static. Foster bought thirty-five of these sets to take back with him to Toronto. It took him two years to sell them all. By then he was on his way—well, almost on his way—as a radio voice himself.

But first he set out to learn everything about radio that he could. He hunted around and came up with a summer job at the Canadian Independent Telephone Com-

22

pany, headed by an internationally known radio engineer, Doctor C.A. Culver.

Foster's job was no soft touch. His alarm went off at five. By five-thirty he'd be on his bike for a long ride west across the city to start work at six. Under Culver's direction he helped make radios in three sizes: one-tube, two-tube and three-tube. The working day ended at 5:00 P.M., eleven hours after starting time. The pay was 25 cents an hour, or $2.75 a day.

He impressed Culver enough that when he quit a few months later, the good doctor dangled a heady thirty-five cents an hour before him as an inducement to stay. But his next move, the one he was leaving Culver for, started his real career. W.A. helped steer him to it. Joe Atkinson, it turned out, had his own version of the radio bug. To gain an edge in that era of red-hot newspaper competition, he decided to promote the *Star* by radio. Furthermore, he decided to do so by starting his own radio station, the first publisher in the country to do so. He began looking for someone who knew about radio and radios and who knew enough about newspapers to earn his keep as a reporter while the radio station developed.

Foster heard about the job opening from his father. Instantly he quit making radios and dropped out of university. He made those moves *before* applying for the *Star* job. When he stood in front of the *Star* executive who was doing the hiring, Foster said he could start work that very minute if need be.

As it turned out, another incipient Canadian celebrity joined the *Star* that same week: Gordon Sinclair. He and Foster shared a desk. While waiting for the radio project to get under way, Foster worked—like Sinclair—as a cub reporter, gathering pictures, reporting on fires and traffic accidents, and helping police reporter Athol Gow. Occasionally he was included in conferences about the *Star*'s plans for its own radio station, but meanwhile he had to pull his weight. Also, he was told, even when the broadcasting did start, he'd still be working a normal shift as a reporter most of the time.

Then the wheels started to turn. First, Joe Atkinson

23

ordered a warm-up period. Readers were titillated daily with news of radio before they were let in on the big secret: that the *Star* was going into the radio business. "We have had the first phonograph," one promo trumpeted, "the first electric car, the first automobile, the first wireless telegraph, the first moving picture, the first aeroplane. People are now asking, 'What else new can there be?' Now comes radio. Just as moving pictures have brought all the world to our eyes, so the wireless telephone will bring all the world to our ears."

And another: "Without wires, except for those attached locally to transmitting and receiving sets, the ticking sound of a clock and watch have been successfully transmitted from Toronto to Hamilton."

Then came the climax: a front-page notice that on the evening of 28 March 1922, the *Star* would present a free radio concert. People could gather in the Masonic Temple at the corner of Davenport Road and Yonge Street and hear a band concert broadcast from more than two miles away. The same program would be heard simultaneously in the Christie Street Military Hospital, a mile or so to the west.

Rain was falling hard on the evening of the concert, but when the doors at the Masonic Temple opened at 7:30 P.M., two-block-long lineups pushed forward. Soon every seat was filled. Extra chairs were hurried in. When eleven hundred were in their seats, several hundred still were milling around outside hoping for standing room. At 8:00, J.R. Bone, the *Star*'s managing editor (no underling would do for a job like this), mounted the stage and assured the crowd that the horn they could see was simply a magnifying device so that the music could be heard throughout the auditorium. This was explained, one assumes, in case some unbeliever might think that a little man was under the stage winding a gramophone.

Where was Foster? He was at the heart of things, at the production center. His nighttime job for the *Star* was as a radio engineer. That evening he was a very nervous one. For the occasion he had been reunited with his mentor, Doctor Culver. The "studio" was on the top floor of the Canadian General Electric Company on Wallace Avenue, not far from Dufferin Street. The radio station handling this pioneering program was Culver's own, the Canadian Independent Telephone Company, call letters 9AH.

The names on the program's talent list were much more famous in Toronto then than Foster Hewitt's: Boris Hambourg, cellist; Albert Guerreo, pianist; Henry Czaplinski, violinist; Evelyn Chelew Kemp, pianist; Victor Edmunds, tenor; Mrs. R. J. Dilworth, soprano; and Romanelli's Orchestra. All had been engaged and assembled without publicity, as part of the surprise.

As master of ceremonies, Doctor Culver introduced the artists. After each little welcoming speech, Foster later recalled, "each performer bravely approached the wooden funnel of the transmission apparatus and sang or played."

Was it a success? Foster was at the paper the next morning when the news began to come in from the *Star*'s far-flung correspondents. The concert had been heard not only in Toronto, it turned out, but in London, Ontario, Owen Sound, Haliburton and Belleville, and in Buffalo and Rochester, New York. It was the first live radio entertainment ever broadcast in Canada and one of the first anywhere. The *Star,* noted lover of good music, was off and running. Concert followed concert, all with Foster at the controls, as he was for the next step, in which programs of dance music were broadcast into halls where the *Star* installed receiving sets.

In all this, Foster must have been doing a lot of things right. Thirteen days after the first concert, he was appointed editor of the *Star*'s section headed "Radio Department." He was nineteen years old.

The listings indicate that only three stations could be heard in the Toronto area. Station KDKA in Pittsburgh would have, at 12:30 PM, a special Lenten church service; at 8:00 P.M. a talk entitled "The Bird Citizens of Pittsburgh" by a member of the Audubon Society; at 8:30 P.M. a musical concert by the Tuesday Musical Club Composers. Station WJZ in Newark had, starting at 7:00 and ending at

10:00, a story called "Man in the Moon," a talk about tuberculosis, a concert by the Scottish Harmonic Association and a recital by a lady harpist. Station WGY Schenectady's evening schedule had one item: a musical program, "Eleven Numbers."

But for the *Star,* in its prophetic enthusiasm, this meagre fare and its own plans were enough to support a radio department. Foster's first run at his new radio editor's job, published 10 April 1922, included a head-and-shoulders picture of a man. The cutline read:

> E.C. MERCER, who has heard the *Star*'s concerts at his home, 8 Royal Avenue, Runnymede, through a simple set which he built himself, employing a clothesline as aerial and the water tap as ground.

ANOTHER STORY WAS WRITTEN ABOUT A MAN WHO, AT HIS home at 921 Carlaw Avenue, heard a Toronto city official speaking to a group of Kiwanians in Pittsburgh. There were numerous stories of that nature, along with single-line items on the radio world: one contractor was installing radio receivers in new homes; an estimated six million people now listened to radio in North America; and so on.

But as most listeners those days built their own sets, Foster's main job was answering letters on how to do it. One example:

> RADIO EDITOR, *Star:* I have a Vimy loose coupler, navy type, with crystal detector, and am fitting it with a vacuum-tube detector; would you give me instructions for hooking up this set, also how long would four dry cells run this tube? ANSWER: See diagram on this page. Do not use dry cells, as they will not give good service with a tube. Secure the usual B battery wet cells, 22½ volts.

THE DIAGRAM, DRAWN BY FOSTER, COVERED TWO COLUMNS at the top of the page.

Among the letters also was a twenty-four-line poem ending:

> Pa put the radio in for me, at least he told me so
> But if it's really mine or not is something I
>   don't know
> 'Cos Pa he wants it all himself to hear the
>   funny things
> And Ma must hear the concerts through when
>   some great artist sings.
> But when the parson starts to talk on Selfish-
>   ness and Sin
> Pa says, "Now it has come the time for you to
>   listen in."

THE *Star* OPENED ITS OWN RADIO STATION ON 22 JUNE 1922, less than three months after that opening concert at the Masonic Temple. Foster became the proprietor, anchor-man you might say, of an early-evening program modestly identified as, "A broadcast by wireless telephone." He would read the latest financial news and closing stock-market reports, the baseball scores and a bedtime story for children, then play a little music. His broadcasts soon branched out to include interviews with visiting celebrities, from a field marshal to a baseball manager.

Station CFCA—Canada's First Covers America!—had its first office right above that of W.A. in the *Star* building. For a while when W.A. tried to call the Bay Tree Hotel, he'd find the phone line was crossed with CFCA's and he'd get band music instead.

By that time, Foster, not yet twenty, was doing everything from editing the radio page to carrying in and setting up equipment for CFCA's Sunday church services. Some listeners thought these broadcasts would ruin churches financially. One letter to Foster read:

> Tightwad Johnson sure did hate
> To see the usher pass the plate,
> Now to church he does not go
> He just hooks up the radio.

Most of the church broadcasts were not from a church at all, but from Loew's Uptown Theatre. In the lifelong friendly jousting between Foster and Gordon Sinclair, one of Foster's jibes was that the only time the church service failed to get on the air was when the broadcast was to come from Walmer Road Baptist Church and Sinclair was assigned to help Foster set up the equipment. Sinclair didn't notice that the batteries were dead. Radio-telephony wouldn't work without batteries. That was Sinclair's last job as a radio engineer. From then on, Foster would go in on Saturday, set up, run tests ("Genesis, Exodus, Numbers"), then return Sunday to announce the service.

But Foster still hadn't broadcast a hockey game, or ever said, "He shoots! He scores!"

4

FOSTER'S FIRST HOCKEY BROADCAST

● ● ●

"In those days the station went on the air when there was something to say, and any stray listener who heard anything whatever wrote enthusiastic letters to say so. There was no such thing as programming."
—Gordon Sinclair, writing about Foster in *Saturday Night*, January 1952

BY FOSTER'S TWENTIETH BIRTHDAY THAT NOVEMBER, HE WAS becoming the most-heard voice of CFCA and at the same time was working a regular shift as a reporter. That summer he covered the courts, wrote special features on the trials of two murderers, and attended the Empire Club luncheons. Between day-by-day assignments he was one of those ready to leave on the run whenever the city editor barked out a command. "Hewitt! Gunshots on the fourth floor of the Ford Hotel!" He was a good reporter and liked the fact that he wasn't in sports, where he'd inevitably be known not as Foster Hewitt but as Billy Hewitt's son.

Meanwhile, Main Johnson, later a senior editor at the *Star,* was assigned to CFCA full-time for many of the organizing duties. One was to assemble the first studio orchestra, fifty musicians under the direction of Reginald Stewart, with Foster doing the dulcet-toned introductions. Stewart was also musical director at the University of Toronto's Hart House and naturally knew how to pronounce composers' names. He was a great help to Foster. Every broadcast was live in those days, with no chance to correct a mangled delivery. Foster always claimed that his experience mastering pronunciations of the names of foreign composers was ideal training for calling hockey games, especially when European teams got into the act.

To Joe Atkinson, hiring halls and sponsoring concerts to plug the *Star* and its radio station was not enough. Such promotions attracted only those people who didn't own their own radios. He wanted to reach the masses, convince them that radio was something they couldn't do without. How better to do it than send that young Hewitt out? Of course, they'd need a truck to carry the radio receiver. A day or two after the publisher had his idea, the *Star* bought its first radio truck—a boxlike Model T of a type widely used at the time as bakers' delivery wagons.

Foster recalled this time in his 1967 memoir:

> The truck contained a coil antenna and large receivers and was tuned to the *Star*'s four-hundred-meters wave. It was my baby. At nights after working my seven-to-five daytime shift as a reporter I drove that radio truck to city parks, beaches, fall fairs, any spot we could gather crowds. Included in my itinerary were Barrie, Alliston, Beeton, Woodbridge, Peterborough, Warkworth and similar accessible [to the CFCA wavelength] centers.
>
> Sometimes the journeys were rather rough. On that trip to Warkworth, my maintenance man and I preferred to take the hilly back roads—and they were really rugged. Along the way we began choking and our eyes watered freely. When we reached Warkworth we stumbled out of the truck and had the gait and appearance of a couple of drunks. Indeed, it was difficult to convince our reception com-

mittee that we were sober until, after some distressing minutes, we discovered that during the drive a large bottle of ammonia had shaken loose and the fumes just about knocked us out. I remember those outings very well for I was then courting Kay [Elizabeth Kathleen How, whose father was a partner in the tailoring firm of Beauchamp and How], who became my wife, and she went along on many of them, certainly for the drive and, I hoped, for the companionship.

Despite the sincerity of our effort, we were amazed at the number of persons who still refused to believe. Especially at country fairs, the skeptics searched in the truck and even under it, expecting to discover hidden recording devices. Frequently someone would say, "How do we know that music is really coming from Toronto? If radio is as good as you want us to believe, why don't you cut off your own program and tune in that band concert over there in the field?" Of course, we couldn't do that, so many visitors remained unconverted.

STILL, THE NUMBER OF RADIO SETS RAPIDLY INCREASED. THE next problem for the *Star*'s radio promoters was to make the programming more exciting. One morning in February 1923, Main Johnson came up with a novel idea. How about broadcasting a hockey game? The idea was put to W.A., the *Star*'s sports editor. He received it with a marked lack of enthusiasm but did discuss it with his staff. They sniffed. Some otherwise loyal *Star* men thought radio was a passing fad. Others thought hockey was too fast for the human tongue to follow. (It still is too fast for some human tongues.)

Nevertheless, Main Johnson wouldn't give up. The first hockey broadcast anywhere took place on 8 February 1923, with reporter Norm Albert as the announcer. The next day the *Star*, in an item written by Foster, hailed this as "the inaugural broadcasting by radio for a hockey game play-by-play."

Albert hadn't stimulated any huge clamor for more, but Main Johnson kept trying. A few weeks later he heard that in Regina on 14 March a game had been broadcast by one Pete Parker. Then Main had an idea: if the sports department was lukewarm, he'd bypass it and send his own by-now-veteran announcer, twenty-year-old Foster Hewitt.

Which meant, Foster said later, "I was the sacrificial lamb."

By then Foster was busy enough with his various general reporting and broadcasting assignments that he'd been replaced as radio editor by Basil Lake. At 5:45 P.M. on 22 March 1923 Foster, who had started work at 7:00 A.M., was chatting with deskmate Gordon Sinclair and preparing to leave when Lake called, "Foster, come here a minute. I've got a job for you tonight."

Foster told Lake he'd had a hard day and hoped this wasn't going to be too strenuous. Lake said it wasn't strenuous, just an intermediate playoff hockey game between the Kitchener team and the Toronto Parkdale team.

That was a moment of portent—which, of course, neither had the slightest notion of at the time. Later, when advance planning had become essential in broadcasting, no one would believe that such an assignment could be left almost to game time. Indeed, it is possible that Lake had tried the sports department and come up empty. But it's more likely that it was (and still is, sometimes) simply the way of the newspaper business. Nobody expects even ten seconds' notice when assigned to cover a fire or a murder, so why should a hockey game be any different?

Still, Foster protested. He'd had a long day. Why couldn't someone from sports do it? Lake said the job needed a radio man more than a sports man. Anyway, Lake added with finality, "This is not a request, Mr. Hewitt. It's an assignment. The late editions say we're going to broadcast the game. And you'd better get up there right away and supervise setting up."

Foster called Kay How, his intended, to tell her the bad news. Then he proceeded rather disconsolately to the Mutual Street Arena, Toronto's main hockey rink. There he bought a five-cent hot dog (his very first pregame meal) and while munching it he tracked down the rink's assistant manager, Andy Taylor.

"Well, let's have a look, Andy," he said.

The *Star* had bought three rail seats next to the penalty bench. On these seats had been placed a glass box about four feet square. Inside was a three-legged stool with six-inch legs and a telephone. The telephone was one of those seen in old movies. It consisted of a box that normally would hang on a wall; on the front of it was a hornlike mouthpiece for speaking into. The receiver, or earpiece, was like a small unbalanced dumbbell and hung on a hook at the side of the main box when the phone was not in use.

Foster crawled in. He wasn't more than five feet seven but even so when he sat on the stool his knees seemed to be around his ears. Thinking his own thoughts, which he later said could be covered by such symbols as "#$%&'()0," he crawled out again and went for another hot dog and a program so he could study the names and numbers of the players. It sure wasn't like a nice orderly church service or a band concert.

About ten minutes before game time he crawled back into the glass box and picked up the phone. There were no dials on phones in those days. He got the operator and gave her the CFCA number. He and the engineer back at the station checked their watches to make sure they'd be operating on the same time. When their conversation finished and the game started, Foster just let the receiver hang and talked into the mouthpiece. For that reason he didn't know until later that every few minutes during the hot action of the game a woman's voice would come on the line plaintively asking, "What number is it that you're calling, sir?"

Even if Foster had known about the interruptions, they would have been the least of his worries. Since his booth was completely enclosed to keep out the crowd

33

noise, the glass kept fogging up. He kept wiping it off but sometimes he could see the skating figures only hazily and couldn't make out numbers or faces. His position was uncomfortable, but he couldn't move much or he'd be too far away from the phone's mouthpiece. He was supposed to talk right through the intermissions, too, giving scores, scorers and anything else he could think of. Then the game went into overtime. He talked a total of three hours that night, including three ten-minute overtime periods. Some time in there, he could never remember exactly when because he didn't know that anyone ever would care, he uttered the four words that were to become his lifetime trademark: the excited, nerve-tingling cry of *"He shoots! He scores!"*

When he got out of the booth he hoped that it would be his last, as well as his first, hockey broadcast. But circumstances have a way of controlling events. At the *Star* the next day letters began pouring in, so many that Main Johnson immediately scanned playoff schedules to see how many games Foster could cover before the end of the season. The excitement that everyone else was feeling then got to Foster. Why not? The letters, the people stopping him on the street, were good medicine for a man of twenty. To celebrate, Foster requested that holes be bored here and there in the glass booth to let in some air.

Spurred by its success, the *Star* looked to other sports. Foster was still down on the newsroom assignment books as a general reporter for the next five years. But at the same time he was broadcasting nights, weekends and sometimes day events as well. On radio, lacrosse, sculling, motorboat and motorcycle races, sailing, dance marathons and football were added to Foster's church services and band concerts, and in 1924 he began broadcasting baseball from Hanlan's Point, the old stamping grounds of his childhood.

Foster usually worked alone, but he and his father got together for one of the world's earliest live broadcasts of a horse race: the 1925 King's Plate. By then Foster was used to making up his own techniques each time he covered a new event, so he looked around the racetrack—then called Wood-

34

bine, but now Greenwood on Toronto's eastern beaches—and set his microphone on a hard chair, which in turn stood on a rickety table close to the judges' stand in the members' enclosure. A cold wind was blowing. Sometimes one of the Hewitts had to grab the microphone to keep it from tumbling off the chair.

There were other hazards. Once the track physician, Doctor J.E. Elliott, left his binoculars on the table beside the microphone. Someone else happened along and picked up the binoculars to glance around. To get a clear picture he had to readjust the focus. In a few minutes the doctor rushed back and grabbed his binoculars to have a look at the field just seconds before the start of the next race. He couldn't see a thing. His angry shout, "Who the devil has monkeyed with these glasses?" went straight into the open microphone and was broadcast far and wide.

Lieutenant-Colonel William Hendrie of Hamilton, a well-known army man and noted horseman, unwarily stopped right beside the microphone to discuss some confidential military matters with a friend. He was chagrined later to find that just about every racing fan in Ontario knew as much about the ticklish military subject as he did.

A few days later, Foster got a letter from Manitoulin Island, at the outer reaches of the CFCA signal. "Who the devil *did* monkey with that doctor's glasses?" the letter asked.

Remarkably little is on the record about Foster's personal life between 1922 and 1925, when he and Kay How married. Or perhaps the lack of personal information indicates the kind of man he was to become. There is something almost wistful about his mention of Kay's presence on the trips they made in the *Star's* radio truck: "She went along on many of them, certainly for the drive and, I hoped, for the companionship." That doesn't sound like a confident swain. They had, however, known one another from their teens: Kay at Bishop Strachan School and Foster at Upper Canada College. The students at the two schools tended to look to one another for dates when a formal or other school functions came up. Foster was a good dancer, light on his feet; he made friends and even admirers easily. (Gordon Sinclair, his deskmate, was a friend for life.)

Kay's family lived in Forest Hill Village, where homes tend to be large and comfortable. She was slightly taller than Foster and as a young woman was slender and graceful with fine, strong features. Both were excellent bridge players. In the 1920s it was common for young couples, married or unmarried, to play bridge on nights when, sixty years later, their spiritual descendants might go to a disco. One may assume from the course their marriage took that they were well-matched in other ways as well, compatible in their backgrounds (a sports editor's family belonged to approximately the same middle-class level as a well-known tailor's family) and, a matter of undeniable importance, strongly attracted to one another in a period, however, when premarital sex carried with it a dreaded social specter of premarital pregnancy, and many made it to the marriage bed not knowing except by hearsay precisely what was scheduled to happen.

When they first married, they lived on Ava Road just west of Bathurst Street, a couple of miles north of where W.A. and Flora lived when Audrey and Foster were born. Foster and Kay's first child, Elizabeth Ann, was born almost exactly nine months after their 1925 marriage. Once when Bill, their second child who was born in 1928, was doing some of that kind of arithmetic that sometimes comes with puberty and curiosity about parental love, he mentioned to his mother, to whom he was very close, that Ann had been a rather rapid addition to the family.

Kay smiled, no doubt partly from a memory, and said, "Ann was a honeymoon baby."

Bill remembers the three-bedroom house on Ava Road as being small but fun. Behind the house was some open ground where, in the 1930s, the Toronto Scottish Regiment would train. Trenches had been dug to simulate conditions of the First World War, and Bill and his friends often played war there.

Their family life from the first was in marked contrast to that of Foster's parents. Flora had usually accompanied W.A. to the races, fights, baseball and hockey games and other sports events that W.A. was working at, or that he covered for the *Star*. Kay didn't go to many games where Foster would be working. If Foster was working, Kay often had some friends in for dinner and bridge. In the first few years of their marriage, their friends were rarely people Foster met at work; few athletes, promoters or other newspaper or radio people visited their home.

Foster's work was fairly unrelenting in those days, and some of his experiences were hair-raising. One that he remembered for the rest of his life occurred one wintry November Saturday in 1926 at a college football game. Toronto was playing Queen's at Richardson Stadium in Kingston. Broadcasting facilities were still nonexistent; the standard press box was a half-dozen straight chairs set behind a folding table near the timer's bench at field level. But field level didn't have the right sight lines for broadcasting. That day Foster decided that his best vantage point would be a perch upon the grandstand's tin roof.

Getting there was no cinch. The first requirement was a thirty-foot ladder. A groundskeeper provided that. When Foster got to the top he found that was just the beginning. He was facing an uphill slope of forty degrees, enough to make most people or objects slide downhill fairly rapidly.

Then there was the problem of getting the broadcasting equipment into place. Foster had to climb the ladder five times carrying his equipment. The batteries alone weighed fifty pounds. At the top he handed his load to his helper who manhandled the loads up to the roof's peak.

Finally they had everything up, including a massive microphone. Then all Foster had to do was slide down the other side of the roof so he could see the field. He fastened a wire cable around his waist, handed the end to his engineer, and slid down the roof until his feet rested on the eaves.

He was there when the game started, feet in the eaves, microphone in hand, scarf tight around his neck, homburg hat solidly on his head. "Not like being in a downy armchair," he said later. "But okay."

Okay, that is, until he began calling the game. Then rain began to fall heavily. In minutes he was drenched, but what could he do? Keep on calling the play-by-play, obviously. In the next hour the weather got worse. Hail hammering on the tin roof almost drowned out his voice and a rapid drop in the temperature didn't help, either. He had to skip the intermission interviews that day. Nobody was nuts enough to follow him to the roof. So he talked through the intermission, did the second half, gave a big sigh of relief and tried to pull himself back up the roof. He couldn't move. He was frozen to the tin roof.

His one-man crew summoned help. They tried to pull him loose by yanking on his safety cable. This worked—but not perfectly. They recovered Foster all right, but the seat of his pants and part of his overcoat stayed behind, stuck to the roof. The rest of the trip up the roof with nothing between him and the icy metal but his underwear was quite funny by the time he told the story to his grandchildren.

He counted one other football game as being worse. That was between Ottawa and the Toronto Argonauts in 1930. Radio had become enough of an influence in sports by then that the broadcast was blacked out in Toronto, but not in Ottawa and Montreal. As usual, he gave the game his descriptive, exciting best. At halftime he interviewed the usual array of distinguished guests. It was not until five minutes from the final whistle that he learned he had been talking to nobody. Somebody had goofed in a big way; the broadcast's Montreal-Ottawa telephone connections had never been completed. For two hours he'd been talking, unheard by anyone more than five feet away.

There were other perils, large and small, in those early broadcasts. He wrote about them engagingly in the Toronto *Star Weekly* for 13 October 1928, getting a spread that would have gladdened the heart of any writer. At the top left corner of his first page was a big photograph of a boyish, rather ski-nosed Foster Hewitt sitting under his homburg hat and above his huge byline. He was casually clasping a microphone that looked somewhat like a pregnant tambourine standing on its side.

Devotees of Jimmie Frise, the great *Star* cartoonist of those days, saw this spread as a collector's item: it was illustrated by four large, action-filled Frise cartoons. All that and Foster Hewitt, too, in a time when the broadcasting world was somewhat younger and a lot funnier.

As a writer, Foster could be mundane or he could be rather eloquent, as he was in the excerpts that follow. He set the scene by recalling his earliest days as a broadcaster, back in ancient times (five years earlier). The prevailing wisdom then was that a broadcaster had to be as close as possible to what he was covering—rail seats in hockey, sidelines in football—so he could identify the players; and set so low that he wouldn't obstruct the view of the paying customers behind him. Hence Foster's first glassed-in booth, four feet high, and its palatial milking stool with the six-inch legs. That was okay for the Mutual Street Arena, but in the springtime of 1923 Foster was in Hamilton covering the Ontario senior playoff between the Toronto Granites and Hamilton Tigers. We take you now to Foster Hewitt:

"In those days radio equipment was very crude. Instead of the complete remote control equipment of today [1928], only the ordinary telephone transmitter was used with the receiver off the hook dangling by your side. I was stationed on the players' bench along the boards of the rink. During the intermission between the second and third periods I started to give the summary." As he did so, Hamilton fans gathered around to shout praise for Hamilton and abuse for Toronto into the microphone. Toronto supporters began to demand equal time.

"Pandemonium reigned! To get away from all this turmoil I placed the telephone under the players' benches, crawled under and completed my preliminary story," which was mainly about how the Granites had dominated the first two periods and had a 2–0 lead, which they tried to nurse when they opened the third.

"The Tigers, urged on by the frantic Hamilton rooters, were in a frenzy. After ten minutes of play they scored their first goal. Spurred on by this success, they scored another two minutes later to tie the game. At this disaster Alex Romeril, one of the Granite players who was sitting on the bench beside me, in his excitement and anger picked up my dangling telephone receiver and smashed it on the boards. That meant that while I could still go on talking I couldn't hear whether it was going out or not. . . . The game ended in a tie but as the Granites had won the first game of the series in Toronto, they took the title." One can almost hear Foster sighing the last sentence of the paragraph: "It sure was a struggle."

Covering the game from the boards, he always ran into the problem of spectators. Once two women were yelling so loudly that they were being heard in Saskatchewan but he wasn't. "I made the mistake of asking them to be a little more conservative in their words of encouragement. It was just like throwing a match into a pail of gasoline." They yelled louder than ever and draped themselves over the broadcast booth so he couldn't see. And then there was the time when fans at an Eastern junior final that had gone into overtime climbed on top of the booth to see better. When they moved around, the whole booth rocked. They also jumped up and down while keeping track of the action. This event was captured in a Jimmie Frise cartoon, full of big guys in derby hats jumping on Foster's roof. In Foster's article he remarks, "As fast as I would turn them away others climbed aboard so that over the radio it sounded like a broadcast of the thundering herd in full gallop. After that broadcast, the booth was nailed down."

At a 1926 football game in Molson Stadium at McGill University, two feet of snow had to be removed before McGill and Toronto Varsity could commence hostilities: "We put up our equipment along the touchline close to the fifty-yard line. We had a long table with the radio equipment on it and I was sitting in a four-foot snowbank all set to go. Just as the game was to start a touchline official called to the referee and pointed to us. He promptly held up the game and ordered us off the field, claiming some player might injure himself against the table. We moved

40

back. That didn't satisfy the officials. We finally wound up in front of the McGill team's bench."

The game was tied 2–2 in the last quarter when Varsity scored its first touchdown, to great jubilation from the well-lubricated Toronto fans. Then McGill, desperate, tried an onside kick, which was blocked, and a Varsity player dribbled it over the goal line and fell on it for a touchdown.

There was no holding the Toronto supporters then. With a minute to go, they rushed along the touchline in front of us, raving like a lot of maniacs. I stood on the table, then climbed on a chair on the table to see over their heads [to describe the last minute of play], but it was hopeless. The whistle blew and the surge of the crowd carried both the chair and myself off the table. It was a wild stampede. But the equipment was unscathed. The next thing was to get Warren Snyder, the Toronto captain, to say a few words over CFCA. I rushed out in the centre of the field where a large mob had "chaired" Snyder. First I yelled, but it was no use. I tried to push the crowd the right way [toward the microphone], but this failed. In desperation I kicked one of the Toronto rooters on the shin and yelled "McGill!" but they didn't chase me. I finally grabbed Coach Ronnie MacPherson and yelled, "Radio!" in his ear. Instantly the word got through the crowd and I had to use what speed I had left to beat the crowd to the microphone. I was out of breath but both Ronnie MacPherson and Warren Snyder said a few words to the radio fans and the broadcast was over.

Foster spent the next two hours cleaning mud off his clothes, then caught the train home. "Thus ended a hectic day in Montreal, which started at 7:00 A.M."

• • •

A couple of weeks later the Canadian intercollegiate final between Varsity and Ottawa (there was no regular east-west university or senior game at the time) was played on the coldest day of the year. Foster, broadcasting from the roof of the grandstand at Varsity Stadium, was bundled up in an aviator's helmet, sweaters, coat and overshoes, and he had two oil stoves beside him. But none of that helped him much to withstand the impact of the freezing north gale.

"At the end of the game I was positively frozen. I couldn't move. I was stiff as a poker. One of the operators, who must have run ten miles on the roof during the game to keep the blood circulating, punched me, rolled me over like a sack of potatoes and generally knocked me about for ten minutes until I could stand on my feet. I sat in the ticket office for more than an hour beside a hot fire before I had thawed out sufficiently to go home. For the past ten weeks of the rugby [which Canadian football then was called] season I had taken turns at getting soaked one Saturday and frozen the next, but had no ill effects afterwards. The following Saturday I took Kay to a theatre and caught a cold that kept me in bed for three days."

He covered baseball from an open perch behind home plate, and once stopped a fast foul ball with a hand that he couldn't move for two days. He covered boxing, horse races and the famous twenty-one-mile Wrigley swims in frigid Lake Ontario, with some of the best swimmers in the world. Foster broadcast these swims from a boat equipped with shortwave radio; he started with a warm-up before the swimmers plunged into the water at 8:00 A.M. When German champion Ernst Vierkotter won in 1927, touching the finish at 8:45 P.M., crowd noise blew Foster's equipment right off the air for fifteen minutes just after he had announced the victor. But his most eloquent account was written about the swim of 1928.

A low-power shortwave transmitter was placed in one of the cabins of Herbert Hatch's yacht, the *Toddy*. Batteries were used instead of a

42

generator. At the press building a shortwave receiver picked up the broadcast from the boat and sent the announcements to the loudspeakers on the shore and over land lines to all the Toronto stations. There was not a hitch in the transmission at any time.

I think the worst experience on the boat was to hear your own voice come back to you from the loudspeakers on shore. No matter where we went out in the lake the voice would simply haunt you. During the dark hours that we followed Georges Michel, the French swimmer, out on the outer course, the voice could be heard coming back to me about four seconds after I had spoken into the microphone, and we were at least a mile out in the lake.

During that long night vigil in the pitch dark, with a cold wind blowing right through us, only snatches of the swimmer could be seen. It was like a dream. The multicolored fireworks at the Exhibition made a weird sight out in the lake. A flash would show two or three powerboats almost touching one another. Another flash and the tricolor of France would show up at the bow of Michel's boat. The next minute our boat would scrape against an unknown craft. To add to the creepy feeling, shouts would pass from one boat to another and on the still waters would echo and re-echo. Above all the noise on the lake, the screams and shouts of happy persons could be heard coming from the midway. Without any warning someone out in the darkness started to sing the "Marseillaise": it was picked up from boat to boat until half a hundred were singing at the top of their voices in a different time and different key. It was a case of every man for himself.

At 10:15, when Michel had gone by the last outside buoy [and I had been broadcasting

43

nonstop for fourteen and a half hours], someone shouted, "He is out!" The twenty or more boats that had drifted practically as one suddenly put on a burst of speed to get a real view of the gallant swimmer coming out of the water. It was like a traffic light turning green. Our boat, due to its quick pickup, pushed by two or three others trying to beat us to it, and was right beside the scene in no time. Suddenly the flares went up for the movie men and it was bright as day. It was hard to see anything after being used to the dark. Michel was all in when taken out of the water by four sturdy lifesavers and rushed to hospital.

One of the most interesting sights during the swim was when the various swimmers were taken out of the water [either finishing or giving up]. In every case a heavy rope was put over the back of the swimmer's neck and under his arms and he was held by one of the lifesavers until help arrived. In Vierkotter's case [the previous year's winner] it took five men five minutes to haul him over the side of the lifesaving launch. Each time they got him to the edge of the boat he would slip back into the water due to the heavy coating of grease and the dead weight. He was as stiff as a poker and had a glassy stare in his eyes as if he was dead.

Vierkotter wasn't dead, but in this report Foster came closer than anyone else writing at that time to communicating what the cruelly cold lake could do to a human in a long-distance swim, the almost superhuman endurance required just to survive, let alone win. Foster contributed dozens of newspaper and magazine articles in the next few decades to the *Star Weekly*, *Maclean's*, *Liberty*, *Reader's Digest* and other publications. This passage on the 1928 Wrigley swim was his best writing.

5

GONDOLA IT HAS BEEN EVER SINCE

●●●

"In the late 1920s there were some Maple Leaf directors who thought we shouldn't broadcast games because it would hurt seat sales. I knew we should broadcast. People who were interested enough to listen to our games on the radio were going to buy tickets sometime, although I didn't realize then that some in later years would travel clear across the country to buy tickets for a team they'd never seen but felt they knew through Foster's broadcasts."
—Conn Smythe's memoirs, *If You Can't Beat 'Em in the Alley*, 1981

CONN SMYTHE AND FOSTER HEWITT MORE OR LESS GREW UP together. Smythe was seven years older, so the Toronto of his middle teens was the Toronto of Foster's boyhood. The Smythe name was heard frequently around the Hewitt dinner table because W.A. Hewitt, secretary of the Ontario Hockey Association, was Mr. Hockey in Ontario when Smythe was leading the Toronto Varsity juniors to the Ontario championship in 1915. Smythe earned his Varsity letter in hockey, and Foster, a few years later, earned his in boxing. In the early 1920s, when Foster joined the *Star*, Smythe was making his living as a gravel contractor by day and coaching, without pay, at night. Foster, as a Varsity athlete himself, was often in the crowds, sometimes tagging along with his dad after a game as W.A. went around to get a quote or two from the fiery Smythe. Smythe coached Varsity teams to intercollegiate championships, then kept his best players together as the Varsity Grads to win the Canadian senior hockey championship. When Conn's Grads represented Canada in the 1928 Winter Olympics, however, W.A. took over the managing job (he'd managed Canada's Olympic winners in 1920 and 1924 as well), because Conn by then was in the early stages of the biggest job of his life.

Through all this Conn and Foster, because of the age difference, had not yet become close friends. But Conn, who always admired the doers of the world, had a healthy respect for Foster. When Conn begged and borrowed the money he needed to buy Toronto's National Hockey League team, the St. Patricks, early in 1927, he instantly changed the name. The Toronto Maple Leafs were born. Smythe named as his first manager Alex Romeril, Foster's old playmate from the night of the smashed telephone in Hamilton. The following year Smythe took over the Leafs himself. One of his first acts was to make sure that the games were broadcast by Foster Hewitt.

Foster was still with the *Star*, but also was getting prestige jobs in broadcasting outside of the *Star*'s CFCA. Network radio was scarcely past the conception stage when he was assigned, by the forerunner of the Canadian Broadcasting Corporation, to cover the arrival of the huge dirigible R-100 in Montreal in 1927. On that one, Foster fed a running account to telegraph operators to be read by Charles Jennings from a studio in Montreal.

Versatility was one of his strong points. When he was sent to meet the *Empress of Britain* on her maiden voyage, he thought one way to beat the competition was to interview two great film stars of the time, Douglas Fairbanks and his wife, Mary Pickford. Running down Fairbanks in the ship's main salon and talking to him first, however, was a major mistake. Pickford, born in Toronto, was the one he really wanted. When he went looking for her, she wouldn't talk. Why? Because Foster had talked to her husband first. Foster complained about this to Fairbanks. Fairbanks just shrugged. "She's often that way," he said.

For the first three years of the Leafs' existence, Foster called their games for CFCA, broadcasting from a spot in the rafters at the Mutual Street Arena. Late in 1930 Conn Smythe was desperately trying to find the money to build Maple Leaf Gardens. Foster remembered:

"One day Conn deplored to me that program sales at Leafs games had not been good and suggested that I plug the programs on my hockey broadcast. He said, 'See if you can sell some to your listeners for twenty-five cents.' I made the pitch on the air and it was so successful that we sold over three thousand copies. This experience convinced Conn that radio, apart from its usual descriptive purpose, had money-making possibilities and so, about a year before the Gardens opened, he asked me to join him in his new enterprise."

Frank J. Selke, Smythe's assistant in just about everything and editor of the Leafs' program, had something to add about the fans' reactions to Foster. In his book *Behind the Cheering* he wrote that, toward the end of the 1929–30 hockey season, Smythe suggested a special program for the fall, to beat the drums concerning the need for a new arena. The program would feature preliminary drawings. When Selke had his program ready that fall, Foster made his pitch one Saturday night. Selke recalls: "On the Monday morning three large mailbags landed on my desk from people sending money, requesting programs and offering suggestions. We had planned to sell thirty-two thousand programs during the season, but had to come up with ninety-one thousand instead."

Smythe got his Gardens built despite tremendous difficulties. Raising the necessary money just then, at the beginning of the Great Depression, seemed impossible. But even as his workmen, some taking part of their pay in Gardens stock, were completing the great building, Smythe was putting together the organization that would make it a success. A major factor was his deal with Foster.

They made the arrangement without a written contract. Leaning on the boards one day at the Mutual Street Arena, they threshed it out. Foster would form a company, Foster Hewitt Productions, to produce the game broadcasts. He would have the power to approve or reject plans for any other broadcasting or filming in the building. He also was to broadcast all events, not only hockey, himself; he would deal directly with anyone wanting to buy advertising time on Gardens broadcasts, collect the money and deduct his own percentage (at a rate he never revealed) before handing over the balance to the Gardens.

In subsequent dealings, he and Smythe did not always agree, by any means. And Smythe lost as many as he won. Which might have been one reason that Smythe, late in life, told an interviewer, "Anybody who thinks Foster Hewitt isn't tough behind that bland exterior has another think coming. He's as easy as pie until you try to push him around. Then, look out! He didn't win all those boxing championships by lying down when things got difficult."

One matter on which Foster didn't have to fight was the positioning and design of his broadcasting booth, which eventually became almost as famous as he was. Construction of the Gardens was still at an intermediate stage when Smythe told Foster to decide where he wanted to broadcast from, and to tell the architect.

Foster knew that when he did so he'd better be right, because if he was wrong he'd have to put up with it for a long time. So, one day in the early summer of 1931, he and Allan Thomson of Thomson Brothers, the building's contractors, spent three hours walking up and down the stairs of a twelve-story Eaton's building on Albert Street, in downtown Toronto. There were windows on each floor. At each window, the two would stop and look at the crowds on the street below.

By the end of the afternoon the decision had been made. From the fifth floor, Foster could pick out a woman with tight shoes and a man with some distinguishing mark, such as pencils in his pocket or an unbuttoned jacket, could lose them in the crowd and pick them out again without difficulty. The fifth floor of the building was fifty-six feet above the street. Foster decided that his broadcast booth would be fifty-six feet above the ice surface.

That same summer something happened that also had a lot to do with the fact that within months Foster's broadcasts became the number-one attraction on Canadian radio. The previous spring, a playoff game between Toronto and Chicago had been played at the Mutual Street Arena, Foster doing the broadcast. An executive with MacLaren Advertising, Einar Rechnitzer, was annoyed at having to cancel a musical program usually heard in that time slot. He was irritated but listened to the hockey game. By the end of the game he was hooked. A few months later one of MacLaren's clients, General Motors of Canada, came to MacLaren's looking for ideas, ready to lay out money if they could find the right vehicle to sponsor.

"Why not broadcast hockey games?" Rechnitzer said.

It was perfect timing. Construction of the controversial Gardens was being rushed (five months was the total time allowed). Games broadcast from the Gardens would get the benefit of all the publicity concerning the building and the predictions, which were split almost equally between those who agreed with Smythe's boast that it would be the greatest rink in the world and those who forecast that it would go broke immediately.

Some time earlier Smythe had called in Frank Selke and Foster. "Go out and sell the radio rights," he told them. Foster had the first bite. He had been meeting seriously with British American Oil Company, Limited, but just when BA seemed sold on the idea, the company got a new president—a baseball fan. That deal had just flown out the window when Rechnitzer phoned and asked Foster to come to a meeting with General Motors.

All hands were jubilant. If General Motors came in, it would be not only a vote of confidence from a huge corporation, but also a hockey first. Other teams in the NHL sold spot announcements for their radio broadcasts, but none had a full-time sponsor.

MacLaren's, General Motors, Smythe and Foster began talks. The terms were that MacLaren's would buy exclusive rights to Maple Leaf games and, for one season anyway, would sell to General Motors regular Saturday-night broadcasts by (it was specified) no one but Foster Hewitt. Foster said later that the financial terms at the time seemed very steep to all concerned, but General Motors eventually said okay to what now seems an almost laughable price: five hundred dollars a game.

C.M. Passmore was MacLaren's co-director (with Morris Rosenfeld) of radio then. He was to produce the hockey broadcasts for the next eighteen years. The first time Foster took him into the completed Gardens to have a look at the broadcast booth, they saw it from across the rink. It looked like a long and slender tube hung in space.

"Why," Passmore said, "it looks just like the gondola on an airship."

As it turned out, the first broadcast ever made from Maple Leaf Gardens, on 12 November 1931, Chicago beating Toronto, almost didn't make it to the air.

What happened was that the original broadcast arrangements had been for a three-station pickup. One would be the *Star*'s CFCA, which by then had moved its studios from the *Star* building to the uptown St. Clair Avenue/Yonge Street area. The second station is unknown now, but those two between them had a thousand-watt capacity. The main station, with five thousand watts, was CKGW, a Westinghouse station, controlled from Westinghouse network headquarters in the United States, which would feed the broadcast to the other two stations.

When Foster reached his broadcast booth, everything seemed in order. He was ready for the play-by-play; announcer Rupert Lucas was ready with the commercials; C.M. Passmore was benignly beaming at his crew. Foster, in his 1967 book *Foster Hewitt: His Own Story*, recalled:

"Alas, we still had some things to learn, and one of them was: don't ever be isolated from the world beyond. . . . All the while we never knew how close the whole operation came to being a first-class flop.

"The villain of the piece was our key station CKGW and it happened in an unpredictable fashion. At the last hour before the broadcast, unknown to our staff at the

Gardens, the American network refused to cancel its usual program and thus clear the air for hockey. That sudden decision was a severe jolt to those in the know [who didn't include the crew at the Gardens] and, after frantic phone calls, they eventually arranged to have the broadcast routed through the Star's CFCA station. Hurriedly the piano team that had been engaged for intermission entertainment was piled into a taxicab at CKGW and told to speed uptown to CFCA. Then, within thirty minutes, thanks to many unsung heroes, a new pair of Bell loops [short lines to carry the broadcast from the Gardens to the station] were in action. The broadcast went on the air at the appointed second."

All this was discovered by the broadcast crew in the third period, when Rupert Lucas went downstairs to the radio control room to see how things were going and came back white-faced.

Foster had opened proceedings that night by saying that he was broadcasting from the Gardens gondola—and gondola it has been to millions of Canadians ever since.

Actually, it was to become almost as infamous as it was famous. At first, it could be approached only by a catwalk without any guardrail, handrail or even parachute. The first time Foster went to have a look he started out bravely, then looked down. "I don't remember my emotions very well right then, but maybe it's enough to say that I went the rest of the way on my hands and knees."

That wasn't all. At the end of the catwalk was an extremely steep ladder, almost straight up and down. Foster went down it, trembling. When he was pulling himself together, he saw a workman approaching across the steelwork from the other side of the rink. He had no handrail either, but he walked upright until he neared the gondola. Then, when he might have used the ladder, he shinnied down an upright and walked across a girder so narrow that Foster got nervous all over again. When the workman dropped into the gondola beside him, Foster gasped, "Why didn't you use the ladder?"

"That ladder?" the steelworker said. "I wouldn't come down that ladder for a thousand dollars!"

Nevertheless, Foster made the catwalk-and-ladder trip

all right from then on. The catwalk was made a little safer by the addition of side cables to hang on to. Still, there were problems. Foster sometimes interviewed celebrity guests during intermissions. One was Graham MacNamee, the best-known American sports broadcaster of his time. He reached the gondola all right, but spent the game worrying about the return trip. George Raft, then a noted tough guy in the movies, was another guest. Foster warned him in advance that the catwalk's height might bother him. Raft laughed that off. When Foster, leading the way, was about halfway across, he sensed that something wasn't quite right behind him. "When I looked back there was Raft, about a third of the way across, hanging on to the wire for dear life. I had an awful job getting him to let go."

Another night, bandleader Ben Bernie stopped at the start of the catwalk and said, "Brother, I know one guy who is not going across that bridge. Me!" One other guest who did make it then made the mistake of looking down at the ice and became sick.

Despite many invitations, Conn Smythe, Frank Selke and W.A. Hewitt never visited the gondola. For Foster, it was soon like home. When people refused his urgings to come see him at work, he used to kid that maybe humans were too far removed from the age when our ancestors dwelt in treetops and swung from the branches.

The height, he always maintained, was essential to his grasp of the game. Long before, he had developed his game-calling style. The gondola perfected it. With only a few teams in the NHL and a mere scattering of rookies coming in most years, he never relied on sweater numbers. To him, Charlie Conacher and Busher Jackson and Joe Primeau and Red Horner and the rest could have worn any number, or no number, and he wouldn't have missed a beat. The great Cook brothers, Bill and Bun, and Ching Johnson of the Rangers, Eddie Shore of Boston, Baldy Northcott, Milt Schmidt, Toe Blake, all of them were as recognizable to Foster from fifty-six feet up as they would be face-to-face on the train to the next game.

People soon began to notice that for some games it was more exciting to stay home and listen to Foster than it was to go and watch. His knowledge of the players, their characteristic strengths and weaknesses, team systems and patterns was such that many first-time visitors found themselves wishing they were not only watching the game, but listening to Foster explain it on the radio, too.

Some years later Ralph Allen, then a pilgrim from the Winnipeg *Tribune* seeing his first Leafs game after a lifetime of listening to Foster, opined in his column that there were really two games in Toronto every Saturday night— the one on the ice and the one Foster broadcast. He had so many letters furiously defending Foster that he later explained he had meant his remark as a compliment. And Foster, perhaps showing in this incident how secure he felt in his way of doing things, finally got Allen off the hook by explaining on a Saturday-night broadcast that the kid from Winnipeg hadn't been all that wrong. A lot of extraneous and sometimes uninteresting things went on in some games, he admitted, but it would bore him to talk about them and bore the listeners to hear about them. He let it go at that.

Foster was then near the beginning of his national fame. In the next decades he became simply *the* most famous Canadian of his time. Perhaps there were people who did not enjoy the almost religious fervour with which radio sets were tuned to Foster Hewitt every Saturday night in the 1930s and 1940s and 1950s, but he was still the most famous Canadian name they knew. The family huddled around the radio on remote homesteads to listen to Foster telling that week's installment of the Maple Leaf story is a Canadian given.

Besides the common memory of family involvement in his broadcasts, there are many thousands, perhaps millions, of individual memories: Foster calling the longest game; Foster MCing the Ace Bailey benefit game; Foster letting his son Bill, eight years old, call a few minutes of a game on "Young Canada" night. The Barren Grounds trapper who would use his radio only on Saturday nights so the batteries would last until spring breakup. The time when no one was surprised to read that six million Canadians, out of a population then numbering eighteen million, had been in Foster's audience on a certain Saturday night. The year that he received ninety thousand fan letters. The time when the present biographer, then an ordinary seaman in training with the Royal Canadian Navy Volunteer Reserve, took part in a survey of mainly eighteen-year-old seamen and stokers asked to identify a list of famous Canadians. Every one in the class could identify Foster Hewitt. But less than fifty percent could put a handle on the name William Lyon Mackenzie King, who then had led the Liberal Party for more than twenty years and had been prime minister for most of that.

Every serious book on Canadian hockey, hundreds of them, has treated the Hewitt phenomenon as part of our culture.

6
THE ROAD TO FATIGUE AND BLOODSHED

● ● ●

"The more I argue with myself, the more I know that hockey today cannot compare with what we once had."
—Foster Hewitt in a speech late in life

FOSTER NEVER THOUGHT THAT THE NEAR-DISASTER ON THE Gardens' opening night would become a benefit in the long run, but it did. Station CKGW was banished from the scene as not being dependable enough for the heady world of three-station hockey broadcasts. Toronto's CFRB, the replacement as key station, assigned a young broadcaster, Wes McKnight, to handle announcements from the ice-level studio. In time he wore headphones and the instant Foster finished his play calling at the end of a period, Wes, listening, would cut in. In time, after the piano duet had long vanished, Wes became chairman of the Hot Stove League, a group of hockey observers who discussed the game during intermissions. Soon, Wes's voice ranked second only to Foster's in recognizability in the huge hockey audience across the country.

Their long friendship and their effectiveness as a team over many decades probably stemmed from the fact that they had worked together right from the start, when nobody in the gondola or the booth even had earphones.

Foster's only book of the time, called *Down the Ice,* showed that his original fascination with the engineering side of radio hadn't faded any. He scarcely mentions himself, except in passing, concentrating for most of the book on hockey rules and techniques. In the final chapter, he details carefully the technical changes the broadcasting crew instituted, sometimes pioneered, in those first years. In that chapter he presents himself as only one of a group of people working toward some kind of engineering perfection. In the end, he sounds more like a cheerleader than the star.

Most of the changes involved techniques that seem so basic, years later, there's a tendency to wonder: why didn't they do it that way from the start? Mainly, one assumes, for the same reason that mankind was around for a while before someone invented the plow. If certain problems of broadcasting were new to Foster, with his R-100 and Fairbanks-Pickford and lake swims and baseball and lacrosse experience, they were new to almost everybody.

In the first few broadcasts from Maple Leaf Gardens, he wrote, the transfer of the broadcast from gondola to ice-level control booth went like this: an operator in the gondola would throw a switch and signal to the engineer in the control room, who informed Wes, who then said, "This is Wes McKnight." No matter how rapidly this was done there would be several seconds of dead air. Years later, this pregnant pause was still being heard in many broadcasts, but not on the hockey broadcasts.

As Foster recounted, C.M. Passmore—called "Pass" by everyone on the crew—simply arranged for headphones at both ends, so that when Wes heard Foster's cue, he'd come in instantly. The same system worked in reverse to get back to the gondola at the end of the intermission, and to improve communications between the Gardens and the bandstand at a dance hall called the Silver Slipper. There John Holden, who later had his own repertory company playing across the country, acted as MC for intermission music. In time, Foster wrote, the whole operation became so mechanized that, "far from feeling cut off from the world, as we had at first, if anything it was too much the other

56

way. What with buzzers, telephone bells, flashing signal lights and a clattering typewriter, it was like doing a broadcast from the city room of a busy newspaper. . . . But [ask anybody on the crew and] they'll all tell you that they would hate to attempt to put out a hockey broadcast today without the intricate network of local loops and head-phones and feedbacks and whatnots to which they've grown accustomed. And to tell the truth, so would I."

Whether the public, engrossed in the game itself, noticed much difference, it was plain that the Gardens, the Leafs, and the hockey broadcasts were on a roll. With Foster's voice as much a part of the team as the players, there had never been such hockey excitement in Toronto as in the spring of 1932, when the Leafs ended their first Gardens season by winning the Stanley Cup. The victory came in a three-out-of-five series with the New York Rang-ers and included one game that Foster forever after called the most exciting he'd seen.

To Foster and everyone else, there was more to this series than just hockey. The Rangers were still substan-tially the team that Conn Smythe had put together for the new franchise in New York five years earlier. But he'd been fired and Lester Patrick installed as manager before the Rangers played their first game. Smythe desperately wanted to get even, and the Rangers desperately wanted him not to, giving the series the kind of extra element that often makes a great sporting (and sometimes not-so-sporting) confrontation.

When Foster talked about the first game of that playoff series years later, he always ran through the biggest names, the stars, almost as if to set up the memory in his mind. The names would roll off his tongue as if each were fitted with a built-in exclamation mark. For the Leafs that year, black-haired and beetle-browed Lorne Chabot was in goal. The great Kid Line of Joe Primeau, Charlie Conacher and Busher Jackson was flying out in front. Red Horner on defense was leading the world in penalty minutes. King Clancy was in his prime in all his specialties, playing, talking, needling the opposition into penalties and just plain enjoying the game. Alex Levinsky, Hal Darragh, Harold (Baldy) Cotton, who years later was a Hot Stove League regular, Frank Finnigan, Hap Day, Ace Bailey, Bob Gracie, Fred Robertson, Earl Miller, all had their devotees. Smythe was manager and Dick Irvin was coach.

Lester Patrick performed both those jobs for the Rangers, plus subbing at least once in goal. His stars were the Cook brothers, Bill and Bun, on the wings for New York's big line with Frank Boucher at center. Ching Johnson, Butch Keeling, Earl Seibert and Babe Siebert, Ott Heller, Cecil Dillon, Murray Murdoch and Andy Aitkenhead were among the Ranger stars.

When the teams skated out in New York's Madison Square Garden on the night of 5 April 1932, more than sixteen thousand were in the rink, breaking the fire marshal's capacity limit. The New York crowd was always one of hockey's rowdiest, and that night they were definitely up for the game. Newspapers had been feeding the fans every extra bit of animosity that existed between the teams. A few years earlier Patrick had decided that Chabot had lost his nerve after a bad eye injury. Smythe had crowed ever since that he'd practically stolen Chabot in return for a goalie he didn't want, John Ross Roach, always soft-pedalling the fact that to make the deal he'd also had to give up Butch Keeling, who had become a mainstay of the Rangers.

Back in Toronto, Foster's dramatic account—still on only a local network—had the faithful on the edges of their chairs. Foster, later, eyes shining, smiling and sometimes laughing at some memory, often used the phraseology familiar to his broadcast listeners:

> Never, before or since, have I seen such tenseness, or such a brilliantly played, wide-open game. The Cooks were tremendous. Lorne Chabot in the Toronto goal was magnificent. Red Horner was knocking them high, wide and handsome on defense. And every time the Kid Line went out there they seemed to be able to take charge.

Along in the second period, the Leafs were ahead 5–2 when Coach Dick Irvin put a rookie Leaf defenseman out on the ice for the first time. Bill Cook went around him like a rocket the first time he came down the ice, and scored. The crowd had been noisy before. But with that goal they let out a roar that never stopped until the end of the period. *And they kept right on roaring right through the intermission!* When the Rangers came out they'd been listening to that roar from the dressing room and it doubled and tripled and quadrupled when they hit the ice.

It set them on fire. They scored again and made it 5–4. But from then on, they couldn't beat Chabot. And near the end of the period Horner, of all people, broke away and scored the Leafs' sixth goal to take the heat off. That game was almost the ultimate in hockey. I'll never forget it.

Perhaps few readers today will recognize those men from the past. Some of them are still around—retired businessmen, some well off and some just scraping by. But then they were the heroes. Some readers, remembering how Foster sounded, will remember the excitement he used to project. And many who knew him well will recall that he never identified personally with another team the way he did with the Leafs team of the 1930s.

One factor might have been age. When that Stanley Cup series took place, Foster was only twenty-nine and most of the players were in the same age group. Also, friends have said since that if Foster Hewitt ever had a hero, it was Charlie Conacher of the early Leafs. The big right-winger with the booming shot was a good choice for anyone looking for a hero. The contrast between his burly, barreling style and those of his line mates, the clever Joe Primeau at center and Busher Jackson, one of the game's greatest skaters, on left wing, was part of it. Just the sight

59

of Busher cutting in from his wing to take a pass and make a shot on goal was, as Ralph Allen wrote after seeing the Kid Line in action, enough to make the hackles stand up on the back of any man who loved hockey.

Foster saw all that, too, but to him Charlie Conacher was the nonpareil. It's possible that Busher's bad-boy habits were too well known to Foster for him to be the favorite. But Foster and Charlie formed one of those friendships that only occasionally occur between a media man and an athlete, and it lasted for life. They were friends in the off-season, too. Conacher later made a fortune from good investments, often passed along to him by hockey fans. Some of the tips he shared with Foster.

One summer Foster mentioned casually to Conacher that he had a tall flagpole to install at his cottage and wasn't quite sure how to go about it. The next day Conacher drove up with King Clancy. Clancy later claimed that although they used a block and tackle it was Conacher's sheer strength that put that flagpole up. It still stands on the eastern shore of Lake Simcoe on the grounds of the summer home Foster built in the early 1930s, when both he and the Leafs were young.

Conn Smythe said in his memoirs that the Kid Line wasn't really that good, that Foster made them national heroes, that he, Smythe, should have broken up the line before he did, but that because of Foster's broadcasts he didn't have the nerve.

And also it should be remembered that although Smythe's judgment was generally good, he did make mistakes. For instance, one time he criticized Foster for always using that line, "He shoots! He scores!" He told Foster he should learn at least four or five more words. A star of Foster's stature today almost certainly would have quit in a huff or gone crying to the newspapers. Foster just turned away, tossing over his shoulder, "Aw, there's no use trying to please you." And went on with what he did so well, including the cry that Smythe thought should be benched for a while. Mentioning that incident not long before he died, Smythe said, "Like me, he paddles his own canoe."

On 1 January 1933, the General Motors Saturday-night broadcasts went on the coast-to-coast network, and Foster for the first time used the opening that swiftly became another trademark, the signal for a nation's rapt attention: "Hello, Canada, and hockey fans in the United States and Newfoundland!"

Now, more than fifty years later, almost everyone on this continent has a vast menu of programming from which to choose. But in 1933, Foster was it, instantly. Many stories written over the next half-century contended, as one said, that "Hewitt was a unifying force, a vital link in the chain called Canada." They were indisputably accurate. He held court from his perch fifty-six feet above a sheet of ice two hundred feet long and eighty-five feet wide, "bringing to life a game with which all could identify." J.V. McAree, one of Canada's most famous columnists of that time, wrote in the Toronto *Mail and Empire* some months after Foster went on the network: "We doubt if any young Canadian ever became so widely known in so short a time as Mr. Foster Hewitt."

All kinds of theories have been projected to explain the Hewitt phenomenon, one being that people in the depths of the great economic depression were the fallowest possible ground for the creation of heroes. And it was true that the spoken voice coming out of nowhere, it seemed, had a much greater impact then than now, when a thousand voices come out of who knows where. It doesn't take much delving to find elderly people who recall weeping on the night in 1927 when they heard on their snapping and crackling homemade crystal sets that Gene Tunney had knocked out Jack Dempsey. People felt such things more deeply then because only a few had experienced the real thing in the flesh.

To begin with, Foster somehow made a whole hockey team come to life in people's minds until the players were as much a part of their lives as their neighbors were. In Winnipeg, when the Leafs beat the New York Rangers in a Saturday-night game, kids used to gather and chant mean things in front of the house where the sister of the Rang-

61

ers' Ching Johnson lived. He, from their own city, had become the enemy. These people had never seen, nor were very likely to see, a game in Maple Leaf Gardens. But, as Jack Batten, a babe in arms when Foster began broadcasting, wrote many years later about the young of that time: "Foster Hewitt, broadcasting in his famous flat, nasal, accurate style, brought them into a relationship with the Toronto players that was as intimate and enduring as anything they experienced in their secret young lives."

Young hockey players had natural allegiances. In Quebec, they wanted to be Canadiens (or Maroons, until the Maroons folded). In Ontario, and especially Toronto, it was natural that a boy would want to play for the Leafs. The rest of the country had been wide open. But after radio, it was no longer. Frank Boucher of the Rangers grumbled years later that Foster had propagandized Prairie and Maritimes kids so much in favor of the Leafs that other teams had trouble dealing with them.

Foster often was accused in those days of favoring the Leafs. He had a good answer. "What I really favor is hockey," he said. "It's the way the game goes that carries me along."

By the 1930s, having left behind the earliest days of trying to shut out crowd noise (the airless booth), as well as the second stage of fighting elbow to elbow with the fans to get his voice on the air louder than theirs, he was in the third stage. Crowd noise rose or fell around him depending on the game. He was like the surfboarder riding the waves: he let the game and the crowd carry him. As the noise swelled, his voice had to go up; when there was a goal and the excitement and noise came at him in a mighty roar, he had to get above that, too. As most of the games he broadcast were played in Toronto before the Leafs' hometown fans, naturally the most noise followed the Leafs' goals. He often drew attention to the fact that in the playoffs, when the Leafs were on the road, the crowd might be nearly silent when a Leaf scored. Then Foster's, "He shoots! He scores!" would be subdued. But when the home team scored, say Boston or Detroit, he'd have to scream the news over the crowd. It all made sense, but some people didn't believe it.

It was then, too, that he developed the sometimes fussy little habits that were to be with him for life, or nearly for life. (The overcoats he wore at first weren't necessary decades later in heated rinks.) He smoked little, if at all, on the day of a game. At one time he used to keep a small bottle of mineral oil nearby as a sort of mouth rinse to lubricate his throat, but some people thought he was swallowing it. A doctor called to say it could injure his health so he gave it up. His normal equipment for broadcasting a hockey game was just himself: Foster Hewitt. No glass of water, because he never felt he needed it— "It's just a habit, anyway." (Some other speakers, of course, use a sip of water to help them remember what they're talking about.) No soft drinks: "Carbonated drinks just repeat and gag you." No food, either. Tension would always ruin his appetite before a game.

And no glasses, no binoculars, no spotter, just his own keen eyes. That was how he started out, and since it was generally considered that nobody could call a game as accurately or keep up with the play as well, he saw no need to change.

At about this time Foster began writing his first book. In later years he sometimes had the help of Henry Roxborough, a veteran journalist and author who was a friend of W.A. Hewitt's, but one must assume that Foster wrote *Down the Ice* by himself. He undoubtedly did get advice on some of the technical hockey points, however. Listed in his acknowledgments were New York Americans goalie Roy Worters and, from the Leafs, coach Dick Irvin, defenseman Hap Day and forwards Joe Primeau and Charlie Conacher.

Down the Ice went into two healthy editions by Christmas 1934, but its popularity wasn't a result of any racy, behind-the-scenes readability. The book reads as if Foster stared himself sternly in the eye and said, "Writing a book is serious business. No jokes." In his reporting for the *Daily Star* and features for the *Star Weekly,* he had shown he could write good observant stuff, but there was none of that in *Down the Ice.*

The author's preface sets the tone: for more than a decade, Foster wrote, he had been privileged to broadcast games of hockey, and during those years listeners had been constantly bombarding him with questions relating to the origin and history of the game. Sometimes he didn't know the answers and couldn't find out.

> But my searching convinced me that the recollections of enthusiasts who knew hockey in its infancy, and who had participated in the transition from ponds to ice palaces, had not been adequately compiled.
>
> Neither has there been much definite effort to present written instruction for the young lads in isolated communities, the eager youth in distant lands or the college coach who has just had the hockey team "left on his tutoring doorstep." Indeed, hockey seemed to me the one vocation neglected by correspondence schools.
>
> So I resolved to assemble all possible data pertaining to the origin and growth of hockey, and to gather playing advice from the masters and distribute it among those who really wanted to "know how."

In short, readers who might have thought they were going to find out what brand of whiskey Busher Jackson drank or what King Clancy said to the referee or whether Red Horner was really a sweet guy at heart when he wasn't knocking people into the cheap seats . . . those readers were out of luck. Although Foster did add in his preface that "the writing has naturally been colored by my personal experiences and observations," that coloration certainly doesn't jump right out and grab the reader. Some of Foster's friends later said if he had a fault it was that he was so opinionated about everything. In his younger days he must have limited this side of his personality to the spoken word. Still, the book is interesting and carefully researched, and qualifies as a primer for anyone writing seriously about the origins of the game.

The book begins with ball hockey, going back to a Greek stone carving dated 478 B.C.; moves up to a line or two about the Irish version, called "hurley" or "hurling," which originally was played with a brass ball (the better to maim your opponent with); then briefly mentions the game native North Americans played. An illustration showed a hockey stick made from a reindeer leg and bone balls etched with speed emblems—a deer on one, a goose on another. It was played in England as well, Foster writes with unjocklike erudition: "In Macaulay's acid account of John Bunyan we find that his worst sins were playing hockey on Sundays and certain musical exercises, which included bell-ringing and fiddling."

This and later historical chapters range from games played more than a century ago in Kingston and Montreal, to those in the early part of this century, to more contemporary (1934) aspects of the game, including the fact that for the final game of the 1934 Detroit-Toronto playoff series seventy-two percent of radio sets in Canada were tuned in. But then he gets down to business: "Rules of the Game" take up twenty-five pages, mainly small type. Then there are passages on how to play each position, a chapter on refrigeration, one called "Did You Know," which is in effect a collection of hockey trivia of the time and one called "Development of Players."

One is relieved to find that coaches, then as now, tend to dream impossible dreams. Foster asked one coach, whom he did not name, to give him the qualifications of an ideal prospect for professional hockey. The coach replied "unhesitatingly" (he must have been standing there just itching for someone to ask):

"The perfect recruit should be physically sound, cool in the pinches, a good stickhandler, strong skater, quick thinker, smart when in scoring position, unusually speedy, and above all have natural ability."

One is bound to wonder what could possibly constitute natural ability that the coach has not already mentioned. But he instantly puts us at ease:

"This latter quality, natural ability, is hard to define," he told Foster. "When I watch a lot of happy youngsters on a pond, I can spot at once that all-too-rare lad who just seems to do everything right, who makes plays instinctively that another would do only after a lot of thinking. Give me two or three such boys each season and I'll look like one swell coach."

At about the time these deathless insights were making coaches all over the NHL wish they had two or three like that every season, too, so they, as well, could look like swell coaches, stories about Foster began to appear in newspaper supplements and magazines.

Films made for theater newsreels showed him looking boyish in the Leafs' dressing room, one foot on a bench as he chatted with players. Other franchises came and went in those years as the league fluctuated from ten teams in the late 1920s to eight by 1935, when the St. Louis Eagles (consisting mainly of the former Ottawa team) bit the dust, followed by the Montreal Maroons in 1938 and the Brooklyn Americans (formerly the New York Americans) in 1942, leaving the membership at six.

Hockey broadcasting was adventurous in those days, since when all the rinks in the league, except Maple Leaf Gardens, were built, radio had not even been considered. When radio came along, room had to be found for broadcasters, and visiting broadcasters were at the bottom of the totem pole. Once in Montreal, Foster and his broadcasting equipment were positioned right in the seats among enthusiastic and sometimes downright wild fans. Heckling and shouted epithets were part of the musical accompaniment, as it were. "In their midst, I was minding my own business, trying to be deaf to nearby voices and endeavouring to talk above the rabble, when something whizzed past inches from my left ear." It was a whiskey bottle (empty, of course). When it broke on the ice, police raced up into the area. Someone, not Foster, who valued his life too much for that, pointed out the bottle thrower. The police sailed in. So did the friends of the bottle thrower. "There was a real Donnybrook and all the while I was forced to continue, even though there was a likelihood that at any time a body might shortly be draped over my shoulders. That was one time I could have used a revolving neck."

Another time, at a playoff game in Detroit, Foster was perched in the organ loft when King Clancy took a high stick close to one eye. Bleeding profusely, he was led from the ice to the medical room. Although Foster reported the events, he was in a difficult position. Reports kept reaching him, some from apparently sound sources, that Clancy had lost the sight in that eye and that his playing days were probably ended. The thought sickened Foster and he decided not to mention anything more on the air until he had a doctor's report.

"Near the end of the game I was describing the play when I heard a shuffle of feet and sensed that someone was standing behind me. I took a peek over my shoulder and couldn't believe what I saw. I took a second look and confirmed that there was Clancy, ghostlike, patched, and weakened from his long climb. He motioned to me to continue broadcasting, then handed me a note that said he had heard the rumors of his loss of sight and asked me to assure the folks back home that he was on his feet and that his eyes would be all right. It thrilled me to spread those glad tidings, for King Clancy, both then and through the years, as player, referee, coach and executive, has been everybody's favorite."

Then there was the long game. These events could not happen today in exactly the same way, because the league learned that night, the hard way, not to end a semifinal Stanley Cup series a long train ride away from, and the night before, the final game was to start.

We pick up the action on 3 April 1933, at the end of the Leafs' second season in Maple Leaf Gardens and a few months after Foster's broadcasts had gone national. He had covered the first four games of the bitterly fought Stanley Cup semifinal between Boston and the Leafs, each team winning two, with three of the four games going into overtime. This was the showdown. The winner would face the well-rested New York Rangers in Madison Square Garden the next night, with the Stanley Cup at stake.

What with the long train rides to and from Boston and the feverish playoff atmosphere, for a week or so Foster hadn't had as much time at home with Kay and their two children as he would have liked. But then at playoff time he rarely did, and neither ever complained about this aspect of their lives. Kay didn't like to leave Ann and Billy alone, so she rarely attended games. The night of the last semifinal game Foster drove downtown alone a little after seven. His bag was already packed in case he had to leave right after the game to catch the New York train.

At the Gardens he walked through the teeming corridors to the Leafs' dressing room. Part of his routine was to check both dressing rooms before the game. Then he could report injuries, lineup changes or whatever when he went on the air. In both rooms the players looked tired from the playoff grind, but some players from both teams assured Foster they were going to get it over with early tonight so they could catch the sleeper to New York. Little did they know. Foster checked in briefly at the control room, then left ice level for the five-minute climb to the gondola and went to work.

The first two periods were scoreless. Foster was in good voice, although the teams were playing cautiously. Near the end of the third period, announcer Gordon Castle, who normally did commercials and shared the intermission commentary, left the gondola so that if anyone scored in regulation time he could interview the scorers as they came off the ice.

But nobody scored in regulation time. The game started at 8:30, the broadcast at 9:00. At 1:25 A.M., nearing the end of the fifth twenty-minute overtime period, Foster had been talking for four and a half hours through 160 minutes of hockey, one period short of the equivalent of three full games. Clancy had scored a goal in the fourth overtime period, but it had happened just after a whistle and so had not ended the impasse. Since the end of regulation time, Foster had been doing the intermissions alone, and he was still on the air.

Notes had been passed to him from downstairs for him to use during breaks in what, if the teams had been less tired, might have been called action. Foster mentioned on the air that although some fans had gone home, others who had been listening on the radio at home had arrived at the Gardens by car and streetcar to see the historic event. Conn Smythe had told the doormen, "Let 'em in free."

During intermissions players were lying on the dressing-room floors exhausted. "I wouldn't mind doing the same," said Foster. He kept his listeners informed of what was going on at ice level: league president Frank Calder had called Smythe and Boston boss Art Ross together to suggest tossing a coin, or playing with no goaltenders, or anything to get the game over with. The Rangers had refused to postpone the first game of the final, billed to start about seventeen hours later in New York.

Increasingly during the fifth overtime period Foster noticed that his eyesight was sometimes blurred when he tried to focus on the play below. His speech was becoming thicker and his pauses longer, although no longer than those on the ice every time the worn-out players could take advantage of a stoppage in play.

It must have been at about that point that Passmore, listening to Foster on his earphones, sensed something was wrong. He opened the door to Foster's part of the gondola just in time to see him teetering in his chair, seemingly about to fall right off. Foster always claimed that was an exaggeration, but Passmore didn't wait to find out. He leaned far out of the gondola and shouted and waved at Gordon Castle, who was standing behind the Boston bench. Castle saw the signal and raced upstairs and across the catwalk. He entered just as the fifth overtime period was ending. Foster silently handed him the microphone.

Foster said later, perhaps influenced by his own relief at being allowed to shut up for a while, that Castle's fifteen minutes of off-the-cuff comments for that intermission were "the smartest, most colorful bits of descriptive broadcasting I've ever heard—about the crowd, the players, the corridor gossip about how to end the game."

At 1:45, Foster was ready to go again when the puck dropped to start the sixth overtime period. It was late in the fifth minute of that period when (Foster's voice): "There's Eddie Shore going for the puck in the corner beside the Boston net! Andy Blair is on for the Leafs now—he hasn't played as much as the others and seems a little fresher than some. He's moving in on Shore in the corner. Shore is clearing the puck . . . Blair intercepts! Blair has the puck! Ken Doraty is dashing for the front of the net! Blair passes! Doraty takes it! *He shoots! He scores!*"

Foster did not talk for a while after that. He went with the Leafs to their special sleeping car at Union Station, went to bed and didn't get up until four the next afternoon, when the train pulled into New York's Grand Central Station. The tired Leafs, easily beaten by the Rangers—who later took the series—were back on the train again seven hours later. That marathon game was not the longest in Stanley Cup history. The Leafs and Boston played for 164 minutes and 47 seconds, about 5 hours and 30 minutes. Three years later, in Montreal, Detroit's Modere (Mud) Bruneteau scored at 16:30 of the sixth overtime period, at 2:25 A.M., to beat the Montreal Maroons 1–0. That game is still in the record books: 176 minutes and 30 seconds of playing time, 5 hours and 51 minutes of elapsed time.

Foster, at the time of the Montreal game, said: "That's a record they can have. I hope I never break it."

Two memorable nights of another kind came in the following season. On 13 December 1933, the Leafs were in Boston in a very tight game. Lorne Chabot had been traded to Montreal even up for George Hainsworth. With the score tied in the second period, Boston was frustrated by the way Hainsworth robbed them blind through several minutes when, twice within a short time span, double penalties had the Leafs playing two men short. They were at even strength when Red Horner caught Eddie Shore with a stiff check and sent him sliding into the boards. As

Horner took the puck up the ice, Ace Bailey, one of the Leafs' cleanest players, dropped back to cover for Horner on defense. Bailey was looking the other way when Shore got to his feet and charged at Bailey, hit him low and lifted him right off his feet. Bailey landed on his head and was knocked unconscious.

Foster, in his book *Hockey Night in Canada*, recalled:

"While Bailey lay on the ice, Horner skated over to Shore, spoke to him, removed his glove, then cracked the Boston player on the jaw. Shore dropped to the ice and was carried unconscious to the dressing room. Bailey was convulsing on the ice. It was evident that he was seriously injured, and while he was being removed by stretcher, a spectator insultingly interfered with those who were carrying the injured player. Punches were thrown and Conn Smythe hit the Boston fan so hard that he also required medical attention."

Foster called all this faster than he was able to write it later. Smythe was arrested and charged with assault. When he was released at 2:30 A.M., he went straight to the hospital. Bailey's life hung in the balance as doctors operated on his fractured skull. The uproar in Boston soon spread around the league. Smythe stayed by Bailey's bedside, leaving only to demand that Shore be suspended for life, if not longer. Bailey underwent a second operation. A week after the incident, his life was still in danger, but then he began a slow recovery. Five weeks later he was well enough to return to Toronto, but he never played another game of hockey. Horner was suspended for three weeks for decking Shore, while Shore, as Smythe said, "was only suspended sixteen games for putting Bailey out of hockey for life."

But Foster always told that story along with another, about a game played in Toronto two months after the Shore-Bailey incident. It was part of his habit of looking for the good side in everything, even in what might have been tragedy. The league had okayed a benefit game for Ace Bailey, the Leafs against a team of NHL all-stars. Each team sent its best for a lineup that could have marched straight into hockey's Hall of Fame: Charlie Gardiner,

71

Ching Johnson, Howie Morenz, Bill Cook, Aurel Joliat, Red Dutton, Lionel Conacher, Nels Stewart, Hooley Smith and others, some of them retired from hockey. And Eddie Shore, who had requested permission to play in the game.

At center ice, Foster was master of ceremonies. When Ace Bailey came to the ice to present windbreakers and medals to the all-star team, he was greeted by a standing ovation from the jammed Gardens. Conn Smythe stepped up to the microphone with Bailey and handed him his team sweater bearing the number six. "No other player will ever use this number on the Maple Leaf hockey team," promised Smythe. (The promise was eventually broken, but only with Ace Bailey's consent; the number went to Ron Ellis after Smythe had sold the Gardens.)

Part of the ceremony that night was a confrontation between the two principals of the night in Boston two months before.

Foster's account:

"Shore's name was called. The big uniformed and helmeted Boston player and the overcoated, bareheaded, dark-spectacled former Leaf met for the first time since the unfortunate incident. They looked at each other for a moment, then clasped hands and talked quietly. What thoughts they had or what they said was never announced. But the cordial meeting of the two stirred the crowd into wild bursts of applause. It was a tingling climax to an occurrence that might have branded hockey forever. That was a night I like to remember."

7

FATHER AND SON

●●●

"I've sometimes thought about writing a book about my dad myself. I read all these books by people who can't wait to tell about what jerks their famous parents were. Mine would be a little different—about how to grow up in the shadow of a famous father and love every minute of it."

—Bill Hewitt in conversation, 1985

PERHAPS THAT KIND OF SENTIMENT IN A SON FOR A FAMOUS father is rare. Or perhaps it only seems rare because good, kind and loving relationships between parents and children rarely make the news. But Bill Hewitt, who became famous in hockey alongside his father, remembers his childhood as a time of fondness and laughter.

When he was six or seven years old he started to bug his dad to take him to the hockey games. "Dad would say, 'Well, okay, but I want you to do a few things to earn it.'"

The jobs would be things a small boy could do around a house. Bill's first experiences with snow shovels were connected to earning his way to a hockey game. "And, you know, in those days practically all houses were heated with coal, and while the ashes would drop through the grates and could be shoveled out, parts of the coal would fuse together almost like chunks of twisted metal—clinkers. Kids today have never heard of them. They'd stay in the firebox and have to be removed. Dad would be heading for the basement and he'd say to me, 'Come on, Bill, I need some help with the clinkers.' And anybody who ever had to do that kind of job would remember how tough it would be for a little boy to get one of those big clinkers out of the bottom of a furnace. So I'd work away and get out probably one little clinker, and he'd take out the rest."

Then, at the game, Bill would accompany Foster right into the gondola and sit beside him, the way Foster would go with his own father, W.A., and sit in the press box.

"In those days, you know," Bill said, "we'd get up there about eight and the broadcast wouldn't start until nine. One night he said to me, 'You want to work?' I said, 'Sure, you bet.' And he said, 'Well, get down beside me here.'

"A microphone to me in those days was like some kind of toy sitting in front of me and I'd begin to call the game in my little squeaky voice. He'd correct me, tell me I was repeating myself too often, tell me how to identify the different parts of the ice where the play would be, this corner or that, the bluelines, center ice. Of course, this would be going out across the network, not broadcast, but so engineers in control rooms would know the score and what was happening before the broadcast actually started. When it got to maybe fifteen minutes before airtime he'd take over and start calling the game himself, so that when the broadcast did start he'd be all warmed up. He always had done this himself right from the start of the game, but now he got me doing the first part of it."

In 1936, when Bill was eight, during an annual Christmas event, a league game the Gardens billed as "Young Canada" night when seat holders were encouraged to bring their kids along, Foster decided that Bill was ready. He introduced Bill as his guest for "Young Canada" night and let Bill call a few minutes of the game, starting the youngster on the only career he ever wanted—to follow in his father's footsteps.

A year earlier, Foster and Kay decided that they had grown out of their first house. Ann was nine, Bill was seven, and their third child, Wendy, was a year old when the Hewitts bought what was to be their family home from then on. It was a comfortable three-story house on Rosemary Road, in an exclusive Toronto district, Forest Hill. A sun room, lots of bedrooms and bathrooms, nice grounds, quiet street—the house cost Foster fourteen thousand dollars in 1935.

On the second floor, Foster's and Kay's bedroom, with a bathroom en suite, as the real-estate ads have it, took up one side of the house. Across the hall the two girls had their bedrooms and shared a bathroom, while up narrower stairs on the third story was a wide hall and two rooms. One was Bill's bedroom, the other a playroom for his trains, toy soldiers (starting with some that had been Foster's) and sports equipment. The family boxing gloves were kept up there, and when Foster showed Bill the manly art of self-defense the hall between the two rooms was their ring.

Accounts of life in that home stress certain elements that, from the start, the young Hewitts took for granted. Their grandparents, on Kay's side the Hows and on Foster's side the Hewitts, often visited for dinner or bridge. The elder Hewitts were particular favorites with Bill because of W.A.'s well-maintained sporting connections. He would sit with Bill and talk any sport at all: hockey, football, baseball. He and Flora often went to the races at Fort Erie, at Woodbine or at tracks that no longer exist: Long Branch, Hamilton, Thorncliffe and Fred Orpen's half-miler called Dufferin, whose ambience sports columnist Ted Reeve once described with succinct accuracy: "Everything is in readiness at Dufferin for the opening of the racing season—the lawn has been oiled." There was no lawn, of course, but a slanting stretch of asphalt in front of the old stands and the clubhouse, where W.A. would squire Flora, who always wore a big and ornate hat and high-heeled shoes. They would spend the day picking winners and losers, then often would dine with Foster and his family or with Foster's sister Audrey and her husband,

75

Bert Massey. The Hewitts being the Hewitts, the talk was more often of sport than business, politics, religion or the arts.

It was a comfortable family to grow up in and for Foster it was an extension of his own cheerful boyhood. Every night the family sat down to eat in the big dining room around a rectangular mahogany table with ten chairs and two big sideboards. If the children had any difficulty or triumph to report, Kay and Foster would listen and adjudicate if necessary. One of Foster's habits was to spend at least part of each dinner conducting family spelling bees, concentrating particularly on words that young Wendy had trouble with, such as *dismal, bicycle* and *business,* with a reward of five cents for every word the children got right.

In winter on game nights, once dinner was over and Foster and Bill on their way, Kay would have a few friends over for bridge and to listen to the hockey game. Kay was apparently always content to let Foster be the sports figure while she looked after the home and family.

Soon Bill started at the prep school at Upper Canada College. (Ann went to Bishop Strachan like her mother.) Bill was active in sports, and one of the big moments of his week came Saturday mornings when the prep-school hockey team practiced at Maple Leaf Gardens. At the same time, the Leafs would be having their pregame meeting and sometimes a light skate. Bill sometimes talked to his heroes, like Charlie Conacher. To thrill the kids, Conacher would pick up a stick and let go his booming shot, making sure it was well wide of the goal but causing the little prep-school goalie to reconsider any plans he had for a career in that line.

When the hockey season was over, Kay began to prepare for the move to the summer place they had bought on Lake Simcoe at Beaverton in 1930. It was about an hour's drive from Toronto. Each year Kay would spend several days packing everything that was needed for the summer: sheets, pillowcases, pillows and other bedding, trunks of clothing, bicycles, suitcases and kitchen boxes. Once it was all ready, a mover from Beaverton would arrive to cart it all north. When the moving van had left, the house would be locked and the family would take off by car. The children sometimes were taken out of school and spent a few weeks at the Beaverton public school.

From time to time Foster would have to drive in to handle his duties as broadcasting director at the Gardens, but for the rest of the family it was good-bye to the city until September. Kay played some golf, mainly in Beaverton, where for a few years in the 1930s she was president of the local golf club. But when Foster was home they'd ask in some local friends. When they had houseguests, sometimes the bridge game would start right after breakfast and go on all day until it was time for Foster to start his barbecue fire for dinner; he always used hardwood, burning it down until the ash was just right and then calling in the hungry children and adults to line up with their plates while he produced perfectly done steaks or chicken.

To them he was not, except in the abstract, an important, nationally known person. He was Father, and by all accounts he was kindly and conscientious, tough when he had to be but not tough that often. But for everyone else in Canada in the late 1930s he had become a giant, an almost legendary figure.

He always said that he wondered how he would have done if the Leafs hadn't been such an exciting team. Still, the truth was, from 1932 to 1940 they were always in the playoffs and only missed the Stanley Cup final twice (in 1934 and 1937), although they were not winners again until 1942.

But to Hewitt's fans, a season's end result had no reflection in his ratings. He received letters from all over, from a lighthouse in the Bay of Fundy, a fishing trawler on the Grand Banks, a women's college dormitory, a Hudson's Bay trading post far north of Churchill, construction camps, barber shops, a theatre company, a place in northern British Columbia that got mail only once a month, hospitals everywhere, Pomona, California, and one from a listener in New Zealand with a cheap radio set that one night, by a freak of the atmosphere, picked up Foster's play-by-play from a five-hundred-watt station in Chatham, Ontario.

He knew his audience from these letters, writers from British Columbia telling of finishing dinner early on Saturday night to tune in at six o'clock Pacific time, others in the Maritimes staying up until ten to catch his opening, while on Ontario farms there was time to finish the dishes and do the chores before the hockey began. He always insisted that none of this was a tribute to him personally; it was the excitement of the game that got them; if he had been describing "the life of aborigines in a Malaysian jungle," he said, "I soon would have been talking to myself."

His modesty impressed no one, however. A Winnipeg writer claimed that "We Manitobans enjoy two things: a bumper crop of Number One Hard wheat and Foster Hewitt's broadcasts from Maple Leaf Gardens." A Vancouver editor remarked that wherever one went, from luxuriant salons to dingy back rooms, every Saturday night Foster was the man of the hour; he "could run for mayor of Vancouver and win a landslide victory" with the Leafs as his aldermen "and no one would give a darn as long as they played hockey once a week." Once one publication of the time listed, one presumes accidentally, for Saturday night: "Hockey—Foster versus Hewitt."

His letter writers wanted autographs, wanted questions answered, wanted him to take this book or magazine they were sending along to the dressing room and get the Leafs to sign it. From places in the United States, where hockey was unknown except through his broadcasts, they wrote to ask if the puck was anything like a basketball, were hockey sticks like baseball bats or tennis racquets, were forward passes thrown by hand and was it necessary to jump over the bluelines.

Once when he had raised his voice to a shout that he knew would have startled those listeners who still used earphones, he apologized: "I just about blew a fuse that time." People mailed him fuses. One night when he realized he had been wearing his derby hat through the early part of a game when the Rangers were leading the Leafs by four goals, he took off his hat and jokingly told his listeners. Immediately the Leafs came to life and scored six goals to win the game, causing his listeners to implore him to leave his hat off from then on. And to help him remember, they sent him a wide assortment of hat hangers. If he had a cold and his voice was hoarse, he was flooded with cough cures. His mail often included gifts. One night there was a box of rabbits' feet for luck, one for every Leaf player. Foster didn't open that until a terrible smell filled his office; the lucky charms apparently had come straight from the rabbits without benefits of a cleanup.

Some critics gave him hell for the way he pronounced certain words. One didn't like the way he said *re*bound, suggesting that he get it right, as in re*bound*. He looked it up, found the critic was right, changed and was castigated by other listeners for trying to sound like an English professor. One night he forgot to mention Newfoundland in his opening. Newfoundlanders were irate. When Yukon and Alaska listeners thought they should be mentioned, too, he decided against that on the ground that if he included everybody who wanted to be remembered in his opening salutations he'd be saying hello all night.

He could have made a lot of money in speaking fees. He received hundreds of requests every year to attend luncheons, dinners, whatever. He turned almost all of them down. When he did accept, for some special reason, he usually simply invited questions from the audience, answered until the questions dried up, then sat down. He confessed that he was nervous at head tables, that the prospect of speaking ruined his digestion, and added: "I suppose it's a family tradition, for the Hewitts were never orators."

It is difficult now to be sure who his close friends were as his first decade at the Gardens neared its end. Some who knew him then said he had no close friends at all outside his own family. His children remember mainly people who came in to play bridge, not always at times when Foster was there. Like Foster, Frank J. Selke had been at the Gardens since the beginning but their association, while never cool, was almost strictly business, although on many Sundays in winter their families would go skating together.

Frank D. Selke, Frank J.'s son, remembers the skating sessions well. "On Sundays, you know Toronto then, there was nothing to do, they'd roll up the sidewalks. Toronto was closed on Sundays. . . . Well, after Mass we'd load into our old Reo, Dad and Mother and the six of us kids, and we'd go down to the Gardens. Dad had a key, of course, and we'd drive the Reo in out of the cold and go skating. And Foster and his three children often would do the same thing. I remember Ann, a little older than I was, and Bill, about my age—he's the one I got to know best—and a little kid, that would be Wendy. Dad and my mother, whose name was Mary, would skate tandem a lot, they'd probably been skating together for twenty years or more, back to their Kitchener days. Foster would skate by himself, or maybe with Ann, and the rest of us kids would be skating part of the time or hunting under the seats to see if anybody had dropped a quarter. But I remember Foster even then as being a little aloof, friendly enough, cordial, good with his kids, but always with the sense that somehow he was on his own."

These skating sessions began in the 1930s but must have lasted into the early years of the war, because one of Selke's memories was of the high windows being covered with blackout curtains, even though Toronto was a long way from any enemy bombers.

Frank also recalls Foster's separateness in other ways, as well: "I used to go to the Gardens often with my dad on Saturdays. His office was on the same floor as Foster's office, and W.A.'s [W.A. had left the *Star* and became attractions manager at the Gardens]. W.A. I recall as a nice warm person, mussing my hair, kidding with me, but never Foster. It may be that he always had broadcasting on his mind."

Foster did make one lifelong friend in that period. The friendship came about because of a major change in what had seemed the even tenor of his ways: in 1935 General Motors pulled out as sponsor of "Hockey Night in Canada." That year GM Canada had a new president who marked his arrival by saying he didn't think hockey was the best way to sell cars. He didn't care if there was a lineup to replace GM as sponsor; they'd sell their Chevs and Lasalles and long and grand McLaughlin Buicks anyway.

If that situation arose today, the advertising agency would be the one to start hunting for a substitute sponsor. In this case Foster cut out the middleman. His theory was that since he was going to have to work with the sponsor, the better they understood one another from the beginning, the better off they'd be. Foster has written since that GM was "eagerly succeeded by Imperial Oil" but no matter how eager Imperial turned out to be, Foster's first meetings were with another oil company, British American, a Canadian-owned company whose service stations were in hot competition with Imperial's.

Before General Motors had agreed to the original deal in 1931, Foster had negotiated with BA. He had some sort of verbal agreement with them that if the rights came up again, he'd give them a chance. They talked again but couldn't agree. When BA finally, and for the second time, told Foster no thanks, he went over to Imperial Oil. The package he had to offer scarcely needed a formal presentation—it was practically pre-sold—but Foster made the deal and then MacLaren Advertising came in to work out the contract.

At the time, a sixteen- or seventeen-year-old youth, Ted Hough, a hockey fan all his life, had just finished high school and his excellent grades had landed him a job with Imperial Oil. He was attached to the advertising department. When the department later got around to giving him a title, he was known as the accounts and budget control assistant. At the time, the hockey broadcast was a large part of the total annual advertising budget (in the mid-thirties, less than the budget for a single hockey game broadcast today). Hough's job was peripheral, at best, with respect to hockey, but it was enough for him to insinuate himself into the gondola. If anybody asked, "Who the hell's that?" the answer was that he was from Imperial Oil. He really had no job in the gondola. "But," as he explained fifty years later, "the circumstances gave me a chance to *intrude,* that's the right word. Then I tried to make myself useful."

Foster was later to refer to the early changes in the original gondola atmosphere. One memory was of notes being passed to him about goals or assists—that Dit Clapper's goal for Boston was his first in two years, or whatever. That note passer was the intruder, Hough, who by the 1970s was president of the Canadian Sports Network and overall boss of Hockey Night in Canada, the dean (or godfather) of those intrepid souls who deal in hockey-broadcast rights with the saints and pirates who own the NHL. He is also a man who never in his life, until Foster's death in 1985, had a job that was not somehow involved with Foster Hewitt.

A look at Foster's career up to that point came a few years later in a *Saturday Night* cover story by none other than his old *Star* deskmate, Gordon Sinclair. Sinclair had spent most of 1935 in India. He wanted to get home to Canada but the *Star* figured that, because he was out there somewhere anyway, he should stop off in Ethiopia to cover Italy's one-sided war against Haile Selassie's spear-carrying tribesmen. Sinclair argued, was brought home briefly, then sailed back, grumbling, to Ethiopia. But not for long.

> Eventually I decided to sail home to Canada without orders and was quite properly fired.
>
> Seeking work, I landed in the broadcasting gondola with Hewitt where, with chatter and interviews, I did pretty well what the Hot Stove League [was to do later]. It was pretty miserable stuff and after one season I was booted out.
>
> That season provided the nearest I've ever seen to a missed program by Hewitt.

What happened was that, in the second round of the playoffs, the Leafs were drawn against the old New

York Americans in Madison Square Garden. The Leafs won the first game at home, then the teams moved to New York. Sinclair continues:

> In other border-crossing playoff games, Canadian microphones had been packed with the Leafs' sweaters, but this time someone decided to carry them openly. The mikes were seized by American customs officers, who wanted incredible amounts of duty. When Foster and I raised a fuss [the mikes were old and American-made], the customs people got tough and decided we couldn't have them just then.
>
> There were frantic visits to New York studios to see what we could borrow, but we could get nothing but carbon jobs that belonged on cat's-whisker sets.
>
> The day passed in exciting telephone calls and eventually the beloved Pass Passmore, producer of the show, chartered a plane and flew additional mikes from Toronto. Pass, who arrived in a Frank Merriwell finish, brought whiskey with him and that was the first and only time I ever saw Hewitt take a snort before hitting the air.
>
> We aired the show from an iron bucket hung from a balcony while fans playfully pelted Hewitt with orange peels, banana skins and peanuts. . . .
>
> While Broadcaster Hewitt is becoming a legend he's in no sense a [colorful] character. No backslapper or party-goer, he dresses quietly, tosses few bouquets, makes no wisecracks and looks but little changed from crystal-set days.

And gradually, with the passage of time, his first and only intense identification with one group of hockey players came to an end. By 1937 only Conacher, Jackson and Horner were left from the team that had won the 1932 Stanley Cup. In 1938 Conacher was traded to Detroit and finished his career with the New York Americans in 1941. Jackson joined Conacher on the Americans in 1940 and ended up playing for Boston until 1944. Horner retired in 1940. With their departure, that era ended, but the man who had helped make their names household words in Canada kept right on going, stronger than ever.

8

FOSTER, THE LEAFS AND THE WAR

• • •

"Dear Foster, I have just been listening to the hockey game that was played last night in Maple Leaf Gardens. It was the most enjoyable time I have had since I left home."
—a soldier writing from a war zone

ANN HEWITT WAS THIRTEEN, BILL ELEVEN AND WENDY SIX in the summer of 1939 before the Second World War broke out in Europe. The Stanley Cup final was over on 16 April, with Boston beating the Leafs four games to one. By 1 May the Hewitt children were attending Beaverton Public School, Foster and Kay were playing a lot of bridge and Foster sometimes drove into town in his white Cadillac convertible to clean up business and to answer the piles of letters left over from the hockey season.

The summer was remembered by the children as one of the best, swimming and boating with their Beaverton school friends, the gaggle of kids sometimes augmented by visitors from the city who would come for a few days or more. On fine Sundays before Foster started the barbecue fire out near the cedars that kept the place private from the street, the lawn would be set with comfortable chairs where the Hewitts and friends and relatives had a drink

85

or two, smiled for snapshots and talked about horse racing and hockey and sometimes the threat of war.

When the German Army rolled into Poland on 1 September, and young Canadians flocked to the recruiting depots to enlist, Foster, thirty-seven, married, with a family, would not have been a candidate for any country's conscription program. Still, early in that first week of war he was at the Gardens in a planning meeting with Conn Smythe, Hap Day and Smythe's longtime sidekick, Frank J. Selke. Smythe was fuming because Prime Minister Mackenzie King was going through the motions of calling Parliament before sending a stirring call overseas to deal Canada in, as well. He felt that, with the country and perhaps all civilization in peril, hockey should decide right away where it stood.

As the weeks rolled by after Canada, on 10 September, declared war on Germany, Foster was part of almost daily meetings at the Gardens. Indeed, he might have been one of the first conscripts—not by Canada, exactly, but by Conn Smythe. During those weeks while Poland fell and people hoped something could be done to halt the Germans right there, perhaps by negotiation, Smythe wasn't waiting. When Leafs came to training camp he arranged that they'd shape up for more than hockey. They were to report to the Toronto Scottish regiment for preliminary army training every morning. All of them. Including Foster Hewitt.

But this program soon died out, coming as it did long before the government's decision about compulsory military service. Indeed, during that winter and well into the following spring, many were calling it a phony war. Poland was one thing, but even Hitler wouldn't be crazy enough to attack France, safe, so many thought, behind its "impregnable" fortress along the German border, the Maginot Line.

Germany's answer was a stunning end run around the Maginot Line to knock France, Holland and Belgium out of the war. Instantly, the problems were acute. Much of the British Army had escaped, battered and bruised, back to England from Dunkirk in a vast armada of small boats and ships. The invasion of Britain seemed imminent. All the Germans needed was a month or two to consolidate before they crossed the English Channel.

Conn Smythe even then was a vocal advocate of compulsory military service. When Prime Minister Mackenzie King did nothing, Smythe instituted a form of conscription of his own. It is not known whether he discussed his plan with Foster and others at the Gardens or simply presented it to them as a fact; which, Smythe being Smythe, was probably more likely. In either case, a few weeks after the fall of France and the rout of the British at Dunkirk, Smythe wrote a letter to all the Leaf players urging them to enlist in the militia. He apparently didn't feel that any patriotic arguments were required, only facts, including one glancing allusion to hockey. After pointing out that as militia (part-time soldiers) they might not be called immediately to active service and might never be called, his letter continued:

"It is my advice, therefore, no matter what your age or your position as a family man, that you sign up immediately with some non-permanent militia unit and get military training in as soon as possible. The advantages are obvious. In case you are honored with a call to the Canadian forces, you will be ready. If you are not called, you will have complied with military training regulations and be free to play hockey until called on."

His Gardens associates, including Foster, toed the same line—while they and the world waited for the final crushing German blow. It never occurred, of course, because for weeks that autumn fighter pilots of the Royal Air Force, some of them Canadians, hurled themselves in mission after mission at the waves of German bombers bent on battering Britain into a state where an invasion would be a cakewalk. It was called the Battle of Britain, and so it was. The German losses were great and once again there was a pause. But no one could be sure when the fierce German offensive might begin again. In Canada, a wave of patriotism not unmixed with panic took over public affairs.

Strangely enough, one of the first targets was hockey. The attack came not from Ottawa, busy making tardy decisions in all directions, but from Manitoba. Mr. Justice J.E. Adamson, chairman of the Manitoba division of the National War Services Board, took matters into his own hands by refusing passports to six players about to leave to join the Detroit Red Wings. His grounds were that young men who were prime prospects for the Canadian armed forces should not be allowed to leave the country to work in the United States. As simple as that.

When that bombshell hit the front pages, Smythe, Foster, Selke and Hap Day, alone in all of hockey, had a ready reply. At the height of the Battle of Britain, Smythe had sent his troops a brief questionnaire following up his original letter. He wanted from each man the answer to a simple question: which militia unit did you join?

Within days Smythe was able to tell the press that the Leafs had twenty-five players in militia units taking military training. Private Foster Hewitt was among them. So was Coach Hap Day, who had been made a lance corporal. Smythe himself, a First World War veteran who had served as an artilleryman, then a pilot, and after Passchendaele late in 1917, a prisoner of war, already was back in the army as a captain when he wrote those letters.

Still, Adamson's move had stirred up immediate debate. Hockey was high profile and when the public is looking for a scapegoat, it's the big targets they go for. Editors, politicians and the general public took sides. The *Globe and Mail* editorialized that young hockey players should be shooting rifles instead of pucks. An Ontario judge declaimed, "When I read the sports page I see great Goliaths of men in the wrong uniforms. All civilization is at stake and we go on as if we were at peace."

But at about that time some far-sighted people in the military began to be heard. While no one could foresee the needs of the future, they said, the single most popular sport in the country should not be taking so much heat. The Leafs and Foster Hewitt and the other teams in the NHL, along with Imperial Oil, had combined to produce the greatest single national once-a-week get-together Canada had ever known. So hockey should go on. And so should the hockey broadcasts, with Private Hewitt at the

● ● ● *In summer, senior lacrosse was played a couple of minutes' walk from the Hewitt summer place on Toronto Island. Foster, pretty handy with his lacrosse stick, would trot over to join in the warmups. (Hewitt Family Collection)*

● ● ● *Foster and friends on the beach near the Island home, about 1908. (Hewitt Family Collection)*

● ● ● *No. 2 Roxborough East, at the corner of Yonge Street. Foster's boyhood home has since been replaced by an office building. (Hewitt Family Collection)*

●●● In 1922 Foster drove the Toronto Star radio truck to country fairs, ball games and other gatherings, hoping to astound the populace with the magic of radio reception from the Star's station CFCA. Skeptics hunted for a hidden phonograph. (Hewitt Family Collection)

●●● His first baseball broadcast, 1924, from the roof of the Hanlan's Point Stadium, now gone. (Hewitt Family Collection)

● ● ● *Foster, at 23. (Charles Aylett)*

● ● ● *Not a lonely shepherd, but Foster—out on Lake Ontario all day and part of the night, covering the 1928 Wrigley swim. (Hewitt Family Collection)*

● ● ● *The referee at McGill made Foster move back from the sidelines. Then McGill subs pelted him with snowballs. At game's end Foster ran into the milling throng on the field, kicking shins and shoving, then running back with the players he wanted for postgame interviews. (Alexandra Studio Archives)*

● ● ● *Foster, back row left, on skates and carrying a referee's bell. Conn Smythe, back row right. Smythe's Varsity Grads later won the 1928 Olympic gold medal for Canada. (Hewitt Family Collection)*

••• *Portrait, 1938. (Bridgdens Limited)*

••• *The original gondola, with the man who made it famous. (Hewitt Family Collection)*

••• *The Leafs barnstormed the West in the 1930s. Charlie Conacher said the huge crowds that showed up at every stop kept asking, "Where's Foster?" (Goertz Studios)*

● ● ● *In 1940, Conn Smythe insisted that everyone employed at Maple Leaf Gardens take at least part-time army training. A year later Foster was commissioned a second lieutenant in the active militia. (Alexandra Studio Archives)*

● ● ● *In 1945 with war's end near, the Defense Department flew Foster around the country to talk hockey to men and women of all three services and, in Halifax, with merchant seamen as well. (Hewitt Family Collection)*

● ● ● *Also in Halifax, when he dropped in to call a game between* Cornwallis Navy *and* Dartmouth RCAF, *the kids mobbed him.* (Hewitt Family Collection)

● ● ● 1949: *Foster, Kathleen and son Bill at Camp Temagami,* northern Ontario, *on a canoeing and fishing holiday.* (Hewitt Family Collection)

●●● *June 10, 1950: Their 25th wedding anniversary. W. A. and Flora Hewitt, Foster and Kathleen, and Kathleen's mother, Mrs. A. D. How. (Tom Carnegie)*

●●● *February 21, 1951: Foster opened his own radio station, CKFH. (Hewitt Family Collection)*

● ● ● *Four generations in 1953: Bill with son Bruce, Foster and W. A. (Hardy)*

● ● ● *An imaginative ace on the CKFH sales staff, soon to be sales manager, later to become powerful in politics. Keith Davey at 23. (Tom Carnegie)*

● ● ● Foster hamming it up as a Canadian National Exhibition celebrity cook. Nanette Fabray holding the microphone. (Ontario Hydro)

● ● ● Foster would go wherever his sponsors asked, coast to coast. One winter in Kamloops, B.C., he backed his bare behind into a red-hot radiator in a motel bathroom. Unfortunately one of the world's most piercing screams went unrecorded. (Portigal & Ayers)

● ● ● As long as anyone still wanted an autograph, he'd keep signing. This was in Winnipeg, 1954. (Portigal & Ayers)

●●● *The late 1950s, Short-run Ford Edsel, long-play Hewitt. (Hewitt Family Collection)*

●●● *But life wasn't all promotion trips. Gina Lollabrigida lived in Toronto a while in the early 1960s. Her compatriot Johnny Lombardi (right) threw a welcome party. (Joe Gulino)*

●●● *Foster and Ed Sullivan, in town for a sports dinner, gang up on Foster's old desk-mate Gordon Sinclair. (Hewitt Family Collection)*

●●● *Foster thought Bobby Hull was the most exciting hockey player of his time. Hull, full of childhood hockey broadcast memories when he first met Foster, later said, "It was like meeting God." (Hewitt Family Collection)*

● ● ● *St. Patrick's Day 1967, a few weeks before the Leafs won their last Stan-ley Cup: Coach-general manager Punch Imlach, King Clancy, an air hostess from Eire, and Foster. (Hewitt Family Collection)*

● ● ● *Foster's book,* His Own Story, *was published later in 1967. Conn Smythe autographs a copy. Red Horner, between them, was the great Leaf defenceman of the 1930s. (Howard Anderson)*

● ● ● *Three years after Kathleen died of cancer in 1968, Foster and Joan Darlie Lang married—and this photo made front pages across the country.* (*The Globe & Mail, Toronto*)

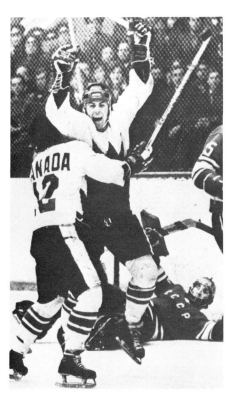

● ● ● *It was the most satisfying goal Foster ever called: Paul Henderson scoring on Vladislav Tretiak in Moscow, September 28, 1972: Canada 6, Soviet Union 5, to win that series for Canada in the last minute of play. (The Toronto Star)*

● ● ● *Ceremonial faceoff, silver anniversary of Hockey Night in Canada. Foster dropped the puck between Colorado's Tracy Pratt and Toronto's Darryl Sittler, then climbed to the gondola to call the game's second period with Brian McFarlane. Bill Hewitt, with Brian, called the first and third periods. That was Foster's last NHL stint: December 18, 1976. (Hewitt Family Collection)*

● ● ● *Joan and Foster, June, 1977, during a celebrity tour of Northern Ontario to promote Canada Day. (Hewitt Family Collection)*

●●● *Foster in January, 1983, under a huge blowup of his favorite photograph of himself.* (Globe and Mail)

controls, even though, as Smythe once remarked, the sight of Private Hewitt in uniform was not quite fearsome enough to stop the war all by itself. Hockey players would not be immune to call-ups, but home-front morale could only be worsened if hockey, one of the national preoccupations, was removed as a way to forget the cares of war.

Once that was decided, things got quite a bit easier for other sports and entertainments. Suddenly they were defensible. Britain itself seemed to agree; sports there continued as usual except when there were bombers overhead.

Foster followed the controversy and its outcome more closely than most. His summation later was that first there had been condemnation of hockey for carrying on business as usual. Then came tolerance. And finally approval, not only by governments and citizens but, more tellingly, from members of the armed forces. The pendulum had swung entirely.

Within a short time, it was difficult for Foster to remember that there had once been some question about his role and hockey's. His work load doubled. He and his sponsor, Imperial Oil, didn't stop at getting a hockey game on the air and then going home. Dozens of war-connected appeals and government announcements went out on the hockey broadcasts.

One of the most dramatic came in December 1941 when the Japanese attacked Pearl Harbor, and the west coast of North America immediately became a potential front line. Canada was badly prepared. Troops were rushed to Vancouver Island, (among them Conn Smythe's Sportsman's Battery, which included a lot of athletes and even a few sportswriters). The RCAF stepped up its coastal patrols. But the whole coast-watching effort was hampered by a shortage of high-powered binoculars. With piles of unfilled Defence Department orders already, manufacturers couldn't cope with the new demand. A meeting on the subject in the Defence Department in Ottawa was getting nowhere until somebody said, "How about Foster Hewitt?"

Not meaning, of course, that Foster might have 500 sets of binoculars lying around, but that a mention on the next hockey broadcast might help. It did. From one announcement the following Saturday night, more than eleven hundred sets of binoculars poured in to the RCAF. Of those, 440 were powerful enough for the purpose. Foster told his audience on the following Saturday night, "That's enough binoculars."

About then also, letters began to pour in from servicemen in England. Some units with powerful shortwave receivers could catch the hockey broadcasts (and would confidently bet on the results with less-favored units). But would it be possible to have them picked up in England and rebroadcast? Foster talked it over with Imperial Oil, which was willing to bankroll the project. Soon plans were made to provide a condensed version of each game to the British Broadcasting Corporation for rebroadcast.

Foster recalled: "It meant long hours, often until four o'clock on Sunday morning, but it was a contribution I really enjoyed. When the Saturday-night game ended I hustled to the radio station, where I listened to recordings of my broadcast. I then selected highlights of the game, especially the plays that resulted in goals. The condensed version was quickly recorded into a continuous half-hour account. Some of the early ones were actually flown to England by the RCAF for rebroadcast there. Later we shortwaved the condensed versions to England and within a few hours it'd be around the world [on the BBC's Empire service]."

Bill, who by then had been with Foster in the gondola every game night from 1936 on (and was to be there every game night until 1950, when he was working at radio full-time in Barrie), remembers those late-night sessions well. Sometimes he'd be allowed to go along, although he was only in his early teens. "The way Dad worked at those condensations is something that always sticks with me. His main thought was, 'What do those guys enjoy hearing about?' So naturally he'd put in the fights, the big body checks, as well as the goals and assists and hometown names. He sort of imagined himself to be where his listeners would be. The worst part was that with the recording equipment used then, if Dad's edited version had even one mistake when he played it back, there was no wiping a bit of tape or splicing like there is now. The whole half hour would have to be recorded over again."

As it turned out, this project couldn't have started at a better time than when it did, in the early months of 1942. The Japanese were overrunning the Pacific, jubilant over not only the terrible slaughter of United States ships at Pearl Harbor but the sinking of two British ships, the battleship *Prince of Wales* and the battle cruiser *Repulse,* with heavy loss of life. German and Italian forces held most of mainland Europe and northern Africa. German tanks, armored cars and infantry were roaring through Russia and the Ukraine. Historians usually refer to that period as "the dark days of early 1942." There didn't seem to be a ray of light anywhere.

In Canada that winter conditions were bleak. Liquor, butter, sugar and some other goods were rationed or very scarce; rental accommodation was difficult to find because of the influx of war workers to the cities; taxes were high. Almost every family had someone out on the Atlantic fighting submarines or flying war planes or fighting or training somewhere. On dark and cuttingly cold mornings when civilians lined up to board crowded streetcars or buses to head to work, there wasn't really much to look forward to. Oddly enough, in all that gloom, a trivial (by comparison) hockey series made a big difference. As the song says, little things mean a lot. Someone who knows hockey only as it is played in the 1980s, with many teams and a long schedule, might find it difficult to conceive of the passions of the old league with its forty-eight-game season that ended on 18 April even if the Stanley Cup went seven games. Which it did in 1942.

Even though the season was only forty-eight games, out of the league's seven teams, six made the playoffs. Toronto finished the schedule second (to the Rangers), and Detroit fifth. But, as Foster wrote at the time, team rosters changed so much during a season then, with enlistments and call-ups, that the final standing didn't necessarily reflect relative strengths. For instance, Boston's top forward line, one of the best in hockey history, Milt

Schmidt, Bobby Bauer and Woody Dumart, were called up in January and inducted into the Royal Canadian Air Force in mid-February.

Anyway, with Foster putting at least one new description into his lexicon—the "dipsydoodle" or its variations, "dipsydoodling" and "dipsydoodler," all used to describe the skating style of center Pete Langelle—the Leafs knocked out the Rangers four games to two in a best-of-seven series that ended 31 March. The other teams played a best-of-three series to eliminate the Canadiens and Chicago before Detroit took out Boston in another best-of-three that also ended 31 March. It was very orderly hockey in those days, which helps one to understand that when Foster talked later in life about the old days, he was referring to something really worth remembering.

The Stanley Cup final between Detroit and Toronto began as a downer for Leaf fans: three consecutive losses, 3–2 and 4–2 in Toronto and 5–2 in Detroit. As Foster reported to the nation before the fourth game, these local disasters had at least briefly distracted Conn Smythe, off at Petawawa army camp taking a course that would qualify him as a major. Smythe had been on the phone to Coach Hap Day. Day had benched two Leaf stars, defenseman Bucko McDonald and top goal scorer Gord Drillon.

Foster's account of the next four historic games, written a few years later for his book *Hockey Night in Canada,* unfortunately does not recapture the high excitement of the broadcasts. But then, what could, in the circumstances?

In the fourth game, the Leafs were in even more desperate straits. They were losing 2–0 in the second period, then they tied the score. They dropped behind again 3–2, but won 4–3 in a game with fights, misconduct penalties, fines and an indefinite suspension for Detroit manager Jack Adams, who charged to the ice in an attempt to attack the referee. Naturally, this did nothing to persuade fans that they should stay away when the teams returned to Toronto for the fifth game. Toronto won 9–3. Don Grosso and young Bob Goldham, only twenty-one at the time, were thrown out of the game for a slugging match they refused to stop. Back to Detroit and the Leafs won 3–0, setting up the seventh game of the series that once had been within a few minutes of being Detroit's in a four-game sweep.

Foster's account:

That game was one of those musts, and the Toronto fans were so enthusiastic over the sensational comebacks of their favorites that the attendance [16,218] was the largest ever to see a professional hockey game in Canada.

The game started carefully. Throughout the first period no one took many chances and the result was scoreless. Early in the second, the Wings' [Syd Howe] scored, and even when the Leafs had an extra man they couldn't dent the Detroit defence. With seven minutes gone in the final session it appeared that the Leafs, after catching the Wings, were about to be knocked off after all.

Forty-seven seconds later Sweeney Schriner poked a loose puck through a maze of skates into the Detroit net and equalled the score. Sweeney added another goal. Then McCreedy backhanded a shot that deflected upwards. Langelle followed its flight, saw it land in front of the Detroit net, swooped [which Langelle did when he was not "dipsydoodling"] goalward and slapped the puck into the Detroit goal before Mowers could move. That two-goal margin held until the finish, and the Maple Leafs became the first team ever to lose the first three games and then rebound to take four in a row and win the Stanley Cup.

Even before the last whistle, Leafs' fans began to celebrate. With seconds remaining, Toronto players pounded the boards, then leapt to the ice, while spectators shouted and cheered. On the ice, NHL president Frank Calder presented hockey's highest award to Major Smythe, who handed it to Captain Syl Apps and coach Hap Day.

For more than an hour fans stormed the Leafs' dressing room, crowded into the corridors right to the street doors and cheered each departing Toronto player.

That was a night I shall long remember. It was a thrilling tribute to hockey's outstanding comebacks, a team with the fight to turn a rout into a triumph.

Because Foster had started his regular overseas broadcasts just a few months earlier, Canadian troops abroad shared all that excitement in April 1942, gathering in the early evening to hear the excitement from the gondola. In later years the question sometimes was put to Foster: would the use of RCAF aircraft to send a hockey broadcast overseas be tolerated today? His answer was, "Sure, given the same circumstances."

He could have backed up this mild reply with a string of official testimonials, but he didn't bother. These overseas broadcasts meant many things to Foster, some little, others big. One of the little things was that on the day of a game he never smoked, to save his voice—but after each game he would get even, smoking to his heart's content, while he put the overseas package together.

One of the big satisfactions was the mail he got. It came from China, India, Australia, New Guinea and Guadalcanal and Tobruk, among other places. He also received telephone calls: one came from the wife of a fighter pilot. She read him a bit from a letter she'd just received about how good the reception was, miles in the air, for last Saturday night's rebroadcast.

For Foster, that kind of fan mail gave him a feeling not every man of thirty-nine had at that time: "I'm doing something for the war effort, even if I'm not in uniform." These rewards for his efforts continued for many years, when Foster traveled the country checking out mining investments or promoting hockey or his sponsor. Ex-servicemen would come up wherever he went: "Hey, I heard you back in . . ." and the places would be Ortona or the Scheldt, Caen or more distant places, wherever the BBC's shortwave signal went.

Foster had an invariable response to the kind of homage that followed him around. He would listen, genuinely embarrassed, and his thanks would always be followed by something like, "Well, it was the hockey that counted, not me, you know." He wasn't comfortable with any other assessment, although once Charlie Conacher, telling about a barnstorming trip the Leafs made one spring after being knocked out of the playoffs, said, "Every place the train stopped there would be these huge crowds, and do you think they wanted to see me, or Horner, or Jackson, or Clancy? No, they'd want to see that scrawny little bastard Hewitt. We'd all parade out and, 'Where's Foster?' they'd say."

There were more official reactions. Doctor J.S. Thomson, general manager of the CBC, made Foster a prime topic before the House of Commons broadcasting committee one day in mid-war: "He brings the authentic voice of home. It can be left to the imagination to realize the exciting and tonic effect of getting actual broadcasts of Canadian hockey matches in a dramatic manner."

The officer commanding the Royal Regiment of Canada, Lieutenant-Colonel Arthur H. Fraser, DSO, was even more specific. He told a civilian audience, "More than anything else, the men in England want the hockey broadcasts, then cigarettes, then your parcels."

During the war Foster got thousands of letters from men overseas. The letters had a sameness. "I was walking past a service hostel right near the Tottenham Court Road tube station and I heard this voice, *your voice,* coming through the blackout curtains and I ran in there and it was the hockey broadcast. I damn near cried."

9

THE IMAGE AND
THE MAN BEHIND IT

● ● ●

"Wartime hockey was an unpredictable mixture of brilliance and mediocrity."
—Foster Hewitt

IN SEPTEMBER 1941, CONN SMYTHE FINALLY MANAGED TO browbeat the Canadian Army into letting him raise his own artillery battery and take it overseas. Before he left, he made sure the Gardens was as well-prepared as possible for whatever the war might bring. By the time Smythe formed his 30th (Sportsmen's) Battery in September 1941, he had instructed both Hap Day and Foster Hewitt to stock up with equipment that might be in short supply later on, and had on file their memos detailing what they had ordered. Foster's planning had to be even more meticulous than Hap Day's because the armed forces were more likely to be commandeering radio and electronic equipment than hockey sticks.

Even after Smythe left on a leave of absence, he stayed in touch from England. His role as team manager he had passed on to Day, but Frank J. Selke took on many of his other duties. There was not, however, a complete meeting of minds between Day and Selke. Both wrote to Smythe regularly, lengthy and reassuring epistles from Selke and terse ones, sometimes reflecting unease, from Day. In one letter Day said he felt that in meetings of the executive committee "there is no one in there to fight for anything." Day, of course, like Foster, had been accustomed to Smythe's habit of putting hockey first in executive-committee decisions. Perhaps it was natural that Selke, a much gentler soul, was unable to battle the executive committee the way Smythe had.

As far as can be learned now, Foster just ran his show and stayed out of the line of fire. This was not, however, as easy as it sounds. Some at the Gardens felt that Foster's original verbal deal with Smythe gave Foster a lot of money that the Gardens directors should have gotten part of. But Foster was never challenged. Although others had built the Gardens, he had done more than anyone to build the franchise into something unique in the country.

He probably had a better view than anyone of what was happening to hockey in wartime. "It included men of call-up age who had been medically examined and rejected [and] unshaven youngsters who still hated to wash behind their ears," he said. "Naturally there was an astonishing turnover in personnel. The Boston Bruins invited sixteen teen-agers to one training camp." Some young players did make the league. One was Ted Kennedy, who was sixteen when he tried out for Montreal in 1942 and was rejected. The following year he went to Toronto in a trade for Frankie Eddolls and became one of the great all-time stars of the Leafs.

Foster didn't knock wartime hockey. He knew it was the best the six NHL clubs could do. To ameliorate the impact of the wartime fill-ins, every once in a while a great player appeared: Rocket Richard of Montreal and Kennedy of the Leafs, to name only two. He also enjoyed the last hurrahs of Busher Jackson, Lorne Carr, Sweeney Schriner, Babe Pratt and other old stars who could still play the game but would have been long gone if there hadn't been a war on.

In the end, Foster always supported the league's decision not to isolate wartime records into some kind of special category, as if they had been set by weaker players. As he was to point out in later years, wartime hockey's records didn't last forever, as some had forecast. Foster could always give chapter and verse to his contention that many players who started in the NHL between 1933 and 1945 could still make the grade when the war was over. But he also could give his cheerful laugh when he remembered some of the lesser ones who played in those days; although when one looks over the lineup of the Leafs who won the last wartime Stanley Cup in the spring of 1945 ... not bad, not bad. Some, like Tom (Windy) O'Neill, who became a Toronto lawyer later, and Johnny McCreedy, who became head of Inco, would have been fringe players at best in peacetime, but others were genuine NHL all the way: Babe Pratt, Sweeney Schriner, Lorne Carr, Wally Stanowski, Ted Kennedy.

Some of those were Foster's traveling companions in the late 1940s. With Conn Smythe managing with an iron hand, Hap Day coaching, Tim Daly as trainer keeping the rookies in their place, and Turk Broda playing his most impeccable goal, Foster orchestrated the national nonstop winter talk shows everyplace people gathered across the land. They talked of Bill Ezinicki's crashing body-checks; the ineffable skating craft of Max Bentley. "That Barilko ain't bad, either." "Yeah, but it's Mortson and Thomson holds the defense together." "Why did Syl Apps want to retire when he and Bentley could've kept on winning Stanley Cups forever?" Foster was the oral historian of his time and much of the country took their themes from his texts.

Near the end of the war and just before the Leafs' surprising 1945 Stanley Cup, Trent Frayne interviewed Foster. Frayne was twenty-six, his eventual national reputation then in its earliest stages. He had been among those legions of prairie kids who listened to Foster every Saturday night. When Jim Harris, editor of *Liberty Magazine*, asked Frayne to do a profile piece on Foster, Frayne went expecting to find a celebrity, but later reported:

> He either doesn't know how, or doesn't care, to play the part of a celebrity. He is as courteous,

patient and sincere with the great and the humble as if he were a rank amateur hoping for a break. . . .

When it is considered that his name is recognized by as many people as Mackenzie King's, it seems paradoxical that he . . . can walk from his tiny office in the Gardens through crowds of hockey fans awaiting the start of a game and, as he makes his way to the gondola high in the Gardens' rafters, no one recognizes him. There is absolutely nothing colorful about Hewitt the Man as distinguished from Hewitt the Voice. The idea prevails that this is because he wants it that way.

Foster Hewitt is not a big man physically. . . . He stands five feet seven and weighs around 140. His eyes are blue and clear, his hair fairish with a wisp of curl and his cheeks pale and full.

Hewitt has often been praised because his hockey eloquence never includes wisecracks or forced humor. This fits his away-from-the-mike character, too. There is nothing of the wise guy or wag about him. His speech leans toward time-tested homespun expressions.

Hewitt's speaking voice is not the voice Canada hears every Saturday night through the winter. Inflexions, of course, are the same, but the volume and energy he puts into his broadcasts are quite different from his normal effortless speech.

Frayne was somewhat bemused by another of Foster's habits, his invariable use of the word *we* where another person would use *I*: " 'We speak from here,' he explains, pointing to the base of his breastbone. 'That's the only place we feel the effects of a broadcast, a dull pain here. The throat has never caused any trouble.' "

Foster invited Frayne to come to the gondola with

him for a Saturday-night broadcast. He watched Foster at work in the small private compartment he had in the gondola. And he talked to him later about some other sides of Foster's work: that he handled all radio advertising from the Gardens apart from the hockey shows, wrote the ads for ice shows, wrote all commercials used on the Gardens public-address system for attractions other than hockey and decided how to spot them at convenient intervals in whatever was going on.

At the end, they talked about television—just looming on the broadcast horizon. Foster had been studying television for two years, he said, and was certain it would replace radio broadcasts in future. Foster's opinion was that, "The camera will catch an area between one end of the rink and the blueline and will move with the play. The announcer's job will be spotting players for the audience, rather than describing play. As the puck moves from one player to another, the announcer will simply identify the players. Television will eliminate a lot of the romancers in radio who don't keep up with the play."

Foster obviously had been watching American and British television, where such low-key commentators were the norm. During the next few years he was to change this opinion completely. When television did come to Canadian hockey seven years later, Foster was the one, the only one at first, to argue that simulcasting radio and television was the way to go, a point he won not only for himself, but for every announcer in North America who called hockey games in later years.

In 1944, when Bill was sixteen, he and Foster got talking about what Bill wanted to do in life. Specifically, what about university? Bill was at Upper Canada College then, in one of the lower forms.

"Dad," he said, "I want to be a broadcaster, like you."

When I said that, Father said, "Well, the only way is you've got to get out in the smaller stations and learn from the ground up. When I feel that you've shown enough interest in what you're doing, and convince me of that, I will try very hard to get a radio station that we can work at together. Maybe in Toronto, maybe not, but somewhere, if you're interested."

At that time, 1944 or so, he said, "What do you think?" I said that's what I wanted to do, I'd start anywhere. He did the negotiating, calling around. I was turned down at CHEX in Peterborough, but then he got in touch with a man he knew, Gerry Bourke, who had station CJRL in Kenora, and Gerry said, "Sure, send him up for the summer. He can go back in time for school in September."

When school ended Father actually went with me on the train all the way to Kenora, more than a twenty-four-hour trip. He could have put me on the train and let it go at that, but he came with me. I can always remember getting into Kenora about six in the morning and the mist was coming off the Lake of the woods and we're walking down the main street of Kenora arm in arm, talking about the place and about radio and about my future. I probably didn't even think of it as being unusual at the time, but I did later, the way he showed me how much he cared about getting me started right. We got breakfast and then he took me in and introduced me to the people at the radio station, and I started at the bottom, emptying garbage cans. Dad stayed around a day, to make sure I had a place to live, and then caught the train back.

In September I came back to Toronto by train. He let me travel alone that time, and apparently he got a good report on me from Gerry Bourke. I went back to school, and to sitting with him in the gondola every Saturday night working the play-by-play.

The following summer he did almost the

101

same thing. First he asked me if I wanted to work the summer in radio again. I said I did. Ralph Snelgrove then had station CFOS in Owen Sound. Dad called him, and Mr. Snelgrove said, "Sure, send him up." By this time I was seventeen or eighteen and I was ready to drop out of school. Eventually they made me the full-time sports director at CFOS, and for the next two years there I got a chance to do lacrosse, boat races, hockey, baseball, softball, trotting races, everything that was going. That was really my baptism in other sports. I always did tapes for my dad, and he'd listen and tell me this and that. And in winter I still came down by bus every Saturday to be with him in the gondola, and the next day when he was home he'd always drive me to the bus, until finally— this was a couple of years later—I moved to CKBB in Barrie as sports director there, closer to home and to the place at Beaverton. At that point he got me a car, a 1932 Ford roadster with a rumble seat. Going downhill with a tail wind I could get it up to about twenty-five miles an hour, no danger of speeding much in that car, which is probably why he got that particular one for me.

Foster's home relationships during that time were virtually unchanged from those of his first years of marriage in the 1920s. His younger daughter Wendy remembers going to hockey games once in a while "but I spent most of the time going out to buy stuff to eat. In the winter Mother was almost always at home on the weekends, and Father was always home during the day." Ann finished school and soon married Frank Somerville. Bill was involved in radio, and Wendy remembers that one feature of her life was the family insistence that, wherever she was, she should not be left alone.

If Kay and Foster were going somewhere together,

Ann or Bill would be called to come over to be with Wendy. "I wasn't allowed even to walk the few blocks from the bus. There had been a rape or something in the neighborhood, and if I was coming home unaccompanied I had to take a taxi or have someone meet me at the bus."

This parental concern was based on other fears as well: kidnapping was a constant fear in families that might be seen as having the potential to pay large ransoms. Also, the house on Rosemary Road was a favorite target for thieves. Nobody in the family recalls now exactly how many times it was broken into, but with Foster's movements so well known through the demands of his broadcasting, and Kay sometimes out as well visiting friends for the evening, the break-and-enter merchants seemed to be competing with one another to see who could rip off Foster Hewitt next.

One night when the family came home, Wendy was first into the house. She ran upstairs to see a man disappearing through a window with that night's haul, which included the medals Foster had won for boxing when he was in university.

The twenty-four-hour concern about Wendy's movements around the city did have one result of which she approved: as soon as she was sixteen, Kay insisted that she should have her own car.

10
PERILS OF FOUNDING CKFH

● ● ●

"I have always nurtured a streak of independence."
　　　　　　　—Foster Hewitt, in *Foster Hewitt:*
　　　　　　　　　　　　　　　　His Own Story

FOSTER ALWAYS WORKED WELL WITH OTHERS, BUT HIS LIKING
for autonomy started with the trips in the *Star's* radio
truck. Then it grew with his pioneering experiences in
broadcasting hockey where, since no one had his experience, he ran his own show and liked it that way. There is
no record of his consulting anyone about the changes he
made from time to time in his professional career, with
one major exception. It is part of family folklore that he
talked to his father every day of his life; the telephone
calls or personal visits were an essential part of Foster's
day right up until W.A.'s death at ninety-one, in 1966.

When Foster left the *Star* in 1931 to join the Gardens,
he was warned by some—including W.A.—that Conn
Smythe was one of the most demanding men anywhere.
But Smythe's assertion that "anyone who thinks he can
push Foster Hewitt around has another think coming"
tells its own story. Foster always spoke well of Frank J.
Selke, who had a lot of say around the Gardens from the
beginning and particularly after Smythe went off to war.

Smythe was badly wounded near Caen in 1944. When he was invalided home, it seemed likely he'd never work again. Some Gardens directors thought this would give them a chance to replace him with the much more amenable Selke, and almost everyone with a big stake around the Gardens was on one side or the other. Except Foster. He kept right out of it.

When Smythe won the battle for the Gardens presidency and Selke made a strategic, and gentlemanly, retreat to found his own dynasty in Montreal, Foster was unaffected. He was undoubtedly the most notable noncombatant in the place.

But all this time, deep down he had one other ambition: to own his own radio station.

As he wrote later:

"There were several reasons for this desire and one of the most dominating [by the late 1940s] was that my son Bill was growing up and broadcasting was in his blood. . . . While he had not traveled the same broadcasting road that I had, he did develop a sound working knowledge and had mastered the broadcasting technique."

Foster wanted to ensure Bill's career no matter what might happen. Even in the early 1940s, when Bill was still a boyish voice beside him in the gondola calling play-by-play before airtime as practice, Foster investigated taking over a station in Oshawa. He decided against that. Then he heard that radio station CHUM in Toronto was looking for a new owner. But two factors held Foster back from that deal. One was that CHUM was restricted to broadcasting only in daytime hours at that time, seriously lessening the station's commercial possibilities. But the main reason for not pursuing that opportunity came when Foster learned that he could only buy sixty percent of the stock. He simply didn't want to put his skills on the line and then have to split the profits of his success with someone else. He wanted lock, stock and barrel. The best way to do that, it seemed by the late 1940s, was to apply for his own radio license.

It was then he found that, while he knew everything about hockey, he didn't know much about politics. When

105

he applied, a rumor went around in Ottawa that he was fronting for someone else who would put up most of the money. The suspicion was that his bankroll came from Conn Smythe, whom the Liberal government of the time had been wearing like a crown of thorns for years. When Smythe had come home in 1944, he had immediately un- leashed a no-holds-barred and much-publicized attack on Mackenzie King for vacillating on conscription. Smythe argued, with much support from other Army officers and even some in Cabinet, that King's policy had caused a grave shortage of reinforcements for Canadian units, cost- ing many Canadian lives.

Smythe had campaigned against the Liberals on these grounds in the general election of 1945. The Liberals won that election anyway, and King later retired. But among the surviving King Cabinet members the most powerful was Trade and Commerce Minister Clarence Decatur Howe. And his job was to accept or reject applications for radio licenses.

He held up Foster's application. Then when Foster was able to convince his interlocutors in Ottawa that Smythe was not involved in his application, Foster showed that he still didn't understand politics. With the Smythe threat gone, he began looking around for office and studio space in expectation that his license would soon be granted. Where did he make a tentative deal? With the *Globe and Mail,* which had some extra space in its downtown To- ronto building. But C. George McCullagh, the *Globe's* pub- lisher, had led the hue and cry over Smythe's allegations against Mackenzie King. Furthermore, McCullagh and C.D. Howe had a long-standing feud over other matters. Howe began to suspect that McCullagh was financing Foster, and once again held up Foster's application.

Oddly enough, it was a hockey connection that came to the rescue. Lionel Conacher, an old Montreal Maroon who had been named Canada's athlete of the half-century, was a respected and powerful member of Parliament. He and another Toronto Liberal sportsman, Senator Peter Campbell, convinced Howe that Foster was not representing anyone but himself. The application finally was approved.

Ironically, Foster's main worry about the application was that the money behind his application *was* all his own. Always careful with his finances, Foster had mustered all his cash assets and had found they weren't enough. He needed another hundred thousand dollars. A bank would let him have it on a loan, but insisted that Foster should put up as collateral all his stock holdings of the time. These were mainly mining shares accumulated over many years, and he hated to risk their known quality and value for a radio station whose profitability was uncertain.

A friend counseled him, "But your station will make money. Can't help it."

Foster said: "But I *know* the value of the mining shares. I might be trading something sure for something uncertain." Bill, with a grin, remembers, "You should have heard him crying."

In the end, he put up the mining shares and was awarded his license for radio station CKFH, a 250-watt station at 1400 on the dial. (The station's spot was later switched to 1430 and much later the power was increased to 50,000 watts.) Foster was happy. Weak as its signal was, CKFH was only the third private station in Toronto.

Gordon Sinclair noted that it was also the only station in the country with its founder's initials in the call letters. Everyone knew what "FH" stood for. Just being Foster Hewitt didn't guarantee success, but it helped.

Foster had everything in readiness. He had decided (perhaps the emanations from Ottawa had made him wary) that the *Globe and Mail* space was not big enough, after all, for his studios and start-up staff of about twenty or so. Larger quarters were available on the second floor of a building on Yonge Street at Grenville Street, about two minutes' walk from the Gardens.

He had also decided where to put his transmission towers. The hunt for the right locations had brought all his old instincts as a radio engineer into play. One condition of his license was that he must not interfere with Buffalo stations, just across Lake Ontario. His signal, weak as it was, could only go north, east and west from Toronto, not south. Some sites didn't fit those specifications. In the end he was happy: he leased some land on Toronto Island, which had sentimental associations, being near the old Hewitt summer home where, as a boy, Foster had caught catfish and captured turtles.

Naturally, a certain amount of publicity had attended all the to-ing and fro-ing among such high-profile people as Foster, George McCullagh, C.D. Howe, Lionel Conacher and others. At the time a young man of twenty-two or so, just out of university, was selling advertising space for some community weeklies in the north part of Toronto and thinking there had to be a better way to make a living. He was a cheerful and outgoing person by nature and one day a friend of his, Jim Service, said to him, "You know, Foster Hewitt's opening this radio station. You should go and work there."

That same day, not long before Christmas of 1950, Foster's office phone rang.

"Mr. Hewitt," a voice said, "my name is Keith Davey and I'd like to work at your new radio station."

It had taken a lot of nerve to make that phone call to a living Canadian legend and just flat out ask for a job. But in those days the matter of how much nerve Keith Davey could summon up, on the right occasion, had not yet become part of the national folklore.

"Do you want to be in the engineering side or in broadcasting?" Foster asked.

"Neither. I want to be in sales."

That turned out to be exactly the right answer. Among the hundreds of applicants Foster had heard from, almost all wanted jobs in either engineering or broadcasting. Foster asked Davey to come in and see his sales manager, Len Smith.

During the meeting with Len Smith, Davey began to realize he wasn't exactly applying for a job at the Canadian equivalent of the Columbia Broadcasting System, which was what he'd figured would be Foster's style.

Smith said, "I'm only going to have one other salesman and I've already hired him from CKEY. If we decide to have a third guy, I'll get in touch."

Keith Davey went back to selling space and didn't hear a thing more "until they phoned me out of a clear sky and hired me. I started on 15 January 1951, and the station went on the air five weeks later."

Foster opened operations with a big party in his new quarters on 20 February 1951, the night before CKFH began broadcasting. His hockey and advertising-agency friends were there to wish him well. Bill, the new station's sports director, was among those listening to the send-off speeches. Bill had left his job as sports director of CKBB in Barrie a few months earlier to be part of the planning along with Howard Caine, the station's manager. Then the real work began.

Two major pluses for CKFH at the beginning were both connected with Foster's past. One was his access to the Leafs hockey broadcasts, which he could carry—not only the Saturday-night games, shared with the CBC, but every game the Leafs played at home or away, which no other Canadian station had.

The second plus was a music program sponsored by the Toronto *Star* and recorded and syndicated to other stations by CKFH. Foster had made a deal with his old friend and boss at the *Star,* H.C. Hindmarsh. Part of the deal was that each program had to be taped and delivered to Hindmarsh to be played and approved as being proper *Star*-type music before it could go on the air at eight each night.

Keith Davey remembers that in the radio-audience surveys of the time every time slot except those occupied by Leafs hockey and the *Star*'s fine-music program showed as an asterisk, meaning the audience was too small to measure. The Sunday-morning church services from Timothy Eaton Memorial Church were popular, but naturally no help at the cash register. On Saturdays the daytime programming was a pioneer venture in ethnic broadcasting; just about every language spoken by Canadian immigrants, except possibly English, was to be heard on CKFH on Saturdays. There were also a number of commercial religious programs available, paid for with cash on the barrelhead. Evangelists and fundamentalists, many from the southern United States and the forerunners of the proselytizers on radio and television today, passed the collection plate from afar by radio. Along with regular newscasts (one by Professor Marcus Long, whose summer replacement was Stephen Lewis), they filled a lot of CKFH air. Also there were the live broadcasts, by Bill, of everything that ran, jumped, skated or otherwise could be called sport.

Davey recalls: "Selling all this was a real challenge for a radio salesman, but I can't tell you how gung-ho we were. I think I was in and out of every main-street store or shop in Toronto in those days, selling time. We had to be pretty inventive. Later we dreamed up something called 'Full-Page Radio,' selling twenty-eight spots a day for a hundred and sixty-nine dollars."

For the salesmen, the weakness of the signal was the main problem. Davey: "Right off the top I made a lot of sales. I sold the all-night show and a couple of major newscasts across the board. I just got off the mark very easily and did very well indeed. Things were flying until at the end of the summer it became apparent that we had a great difficulty. People couldn't hear the station much north of Eglinton Avenue. I remember I had a furrier up in Thornhill on the air. He could never hear his program. What we would do is take a car up so he could listen, if you can imagine that. You could get it in the car but not in the homes. When this became known we immediately were in considerable difficulty. We were very nearly sold out of space by September 1951, but then people began to cancel; I'll never forget it, a real run."

Davey soon became sales manager. He held a sales meeting every Monday morning in Foster's office, which was done in blond wood and included a lot of heavy old family-type furniture. Foster did not attend these meetings. But each week Davey made a written report on sales accomplishments and plans, and every so often had a long session, two hours or so, with Foster. These sometimes took place at Foster's and Kay's home on Rosemary Road.

Exactly how the station was doing financially was known only to Foster, and he characteristically kept his cards close to his vest. But Bill's memory is, "I think we made money from the very start."

Davey recalled:

We had to become very inventive. I remember one time I had a great idea . . . to get a hockey player with a known name working on the station. So some of us cooked up the idea of the morning show. That spring after the hockey season was over we hired Eric Nesterenko to be our morning man and he was just absolutely awful. I remember going over to the Gardens grill for lunch one day, and Harold Ballard [not yet the power he was to become] asked me, "How much is that cheap s.o.b. Foster paying Eric?" and I told him the truth, which was twenty-five dollars a week. But Nester didn't last long, and it wasn't only because of the pay.

Another idea I had, I guess I was sales manager by then, was to get a hockey player to work as a salesman, selling advertising. I remember going after Billy Harris and he couldn't do it and then I hired Bobby Baun. He came with us for several summers. I remember Hearn Buick Pontiac sponsored the six o'clock sports news, which Bill Hewitt did, one of our better shows, and I gave the account to Baun to service. One night the Leafs were playing in Chicago and . . . getting on the train Foster bumped into Baun and said, "What's happening to the Hearn Buick Pontiac account?" Baun said, "Look, I don't have anything to do with it, you'd better ask Keith."

When Foster came back he was quite cross with me because out of this Baun was getting a commission, probably a dollar a sportscast. Foster was frugal.

111

• • •

In those early days, Foster's friends at MacLaren Advertising got together with senior staff at CKFH to work out a broadcasting philosophy. They produced the slogan, "Radio For Grownups," and a new policy. They wanted to get rid of all the ethnic and religious programs and hit the radio market with something new. Everyone was enthusiastic. Davey's sales department was ecstatic. Foster seemed to like it. But there was a little of the penny-wise, pound-foolish in him. He couldn't quite bring himself to dump all those revenue-producing ethnics and preachers just on the chance, however well-recommended, that a new music policy would help CKFH capture the listenerships of the local heavies such as CFRB.

So it didn't happen, and Davey had to make do with what he had. One of his better sales weapons was Foster himself. "Every midweek game, I could take an agency guy up to the gondola to watch the game. It was a great winner. Even the most blasé media director was pretty impressed, coming to the Gardens with me and actually getting into the gondola with Foster. After the game, Foster would have a few words with them."

A variation took place after some Saturday-night games: Davey and Foster took guests over to the station after a game to show them around. Once Foster took the visitors to the basement. "This is our music library," he said, and opened the door on a couple who were busily making their own music.

"Oh, pardon me," Foster said, and closed the door.

11

NOBODY ELSE HAD FOSTER HEWITT

● ● ●

"Before we started to do hockey on television, there was a lot of discussion going on that Foster wasn't really suitable for TV. One reason was, the Americans were televising hockey before we got under way and they always did it on the basis of the less commentary the better. Foster had the theory and I agreed with him, I must admit, that his own commentary just as on radio was a hell of a lot better on television than the sort of almost cricket-style commentary that the Americans were using. I think he really made the television thing work properly. It was Foster's personality that made it stick, his style, his excitement."
—Hugh Horler, producer, Hockey Night in Canada, 1949 to 1967

FOSTER'S INTEREST IN TELEVISION WENT BACK A LONG WAY. In 1931, before the Maple Leaf Gardens opened, he had been invited to New York by the Radio Corporation of America for a demonstration of the new technology: a broadcast (on a five-inch screen!) of boxing and wrestling from Madison Square Garden. The screen was a little bigger a couple of years later when Eaton's in Toronto used television for the first in-store promotion of its type in Canada, naturally engaging Foster as the commentator. The experiment reminded him of his first sight and sound of radio in Detroit, when he was only eighteen.

At Eaton's, Foster sat in a studio on the store's second floor, introducing live musicians and from time to time interviewing sports celebrities on camera for transmission to a crowd of about three hundred in an auditorium on the sixth floor. One of Foster's guests was Australian sculler Bobby Pearce, the 1928 Olympic champion and later professional champion.

Despite this early publicity, radio remained the king of the airwaves until, in the late 1940s, television made its big move in the wake of the Second World War, precisely as radio had burgeoned after the First World War.

From the start, Foster was all for getting hockey on television. Conn Smythe tended to agree, feeling much the same as he had about radio—that it would enhance the game. Some other hockey people held back. Even in 1949, when New York and Detroit were telecasting home games with a lineup of sponsors, NHL president Clarence Campbell was saying that television sets were expensive and could be afforded only by people in the upper-income range—the ones who bought the best tickets to games. "These are the people who support hockey and if they stay home it is estimated that the six NHL clubs could lose a million dollars in gate receipts." He thought it doubtful that television could afford to pay enough for broadcast rights to make up for the lost attendance.

By 1950, Chicago and Boston were televising home games as well, but in Chicago the club made its first sponsor agree not only to pay for the rights, but to reimburse the Chicago club for every vacant seat at every game!

Foster didn't agree with any of the nay-sayers. He bought one of the first home television sets in Canada years before the Leafs games were televised, and found that the set was on every night from dinner to midnight. Watching, and relating what he saw to the prospect of

114

hockey television in Canada, he remembered those old first directors of the Leafs who had argued with Conn Smythe that radio would ruin hockey attendance. Instead, radio had sent listeners to the ticket wickets to see live games. He was convinced television would have the same effect, and of course he was right.

By 1952, when Canadian television began, the people working around Foster were in some respects the most important of his life. Hugh Horler, a laconic, slim, dark young man, was working for MacLaren Advertising's Winnipeg office in 1940 when he first met Foster, who was making a promotional swing through western Canada. In 1942 MacLaren's moved Horler to Toronto and straight into the hockey crew as, he says, "an errand boy for Pass Passmore," who'd produced the show from the beginning. After a few years Horler became assistant producer. His role included writing scripts for what most listeners thought were ad libs during the intermissions' popular Hot Stove League. In 1949, on Passmore's death, Horler succeeded him as producer.

Ted Hough remained with Imperial Oil for a while, but in 1953 was hired by MacLaren as Horler's assistant "to install some order on the financial side." Hough had never really had a sponsor's role to fill up there in the rafters; he had insinuated himself into the gondola originally because he had a good deal of nerve under that obliging exterior, and he had made himself useful from the start. Hough thus became one of the longest surviving members of the 1930s gondola group. He still worked as a spotter of visible or statistical points of interest that Foster might have missed in his single-minded concentration on the play. Hough was a self-effacing person, well-liked, efficient. It is unlikely that anyone at the time—even Hough himself—saw Hough as the future boss of the whole shebang. Only in later years did people realize that one of his strengths was the impression he gave of being non-threatening. He never came at a problem with all guns blazing; he was more inclined to go around walls than over them. These attributes helped Hough to fit in with

Foster (a hero to Hough), who was also quietly indomitable in his own way, Conn Smythe, who occasionally barked orders from the wings, the sponsor who insisted on his prerogatives and the CBC, which fought a number of rearguard actions to protect its autonomy.

The other person to become of prime importance then and later was H.M. Turner, Jr., known as Bud. He was six or seven years younger than Horler and Hough, and had grown up near the Smythes, but hadn't been a hockey buff, although that was not far off. He did have some television experience, however, having worked on the Fred Waring show in the United States. Mainly, he says, his work with Waring had been confined to running toasters and electric kettles in and out of the live General Electric commercials, but in 1952 anyone bright and likable, as Bud Turner was, who also had been close enough to a television camera that he could distinguish it from, say, a fire hydrant, had at least a fighting change for a job in Canadian advertising or television. He soon became an account executive and worked on the Imperial Oil account.

Into this mix one must place, somewhere, the late Kay Dale. From the beginning, she acted as Hockey Night's coordinator both in the MacLaren office and in the gondola. She had a warm and lasting friendship with Foster. If it was more than friendship, as some believed, discretion was total. But when Foster set up a company to handle his holdings he called it Hewitt-dale Productions, Limited, with the "dale" part never explained.

It is impossible to trace the reasons for Foster's complete turnabout over five or six years in how he felt hockey should be handled on television. He made a quite explicit statement to Trent Frayne late in 1944, saying that when television came to Hockey Night in Canada, "the announcer's job will be spotting players for the audience, rather than describing play." It seems likely that when he thought that through he saw that he was automatically excluding himself from the prime job in the eventual move to television. Probably equally important was his realization, when he began to watch hockey as televised in New York, Detroit, Boston and Chicago by announcers using that hands-off technique, that the exclusion of his kind of background information, color and expert interpretation detracted from the excitement the game should project.

At any rate, when in 1951 the CBC decided to target the autumn of 1952 as the start-up time for Canadian television, the people most involved with hockey broadcasting had their own decisions to make. Some felt that Foster's technique was not right for television. Others worried that if another play-by-play man called the televised games, many viewers would compare him unfavorably with Foster as they knew him on radio. At the core of the problem was everyone's awareness that while radio and television talent formed separate units in other rinks, the other rinks didn't have Foster Hewitt. And there was also the fact that Foster was stubbornly insisting that what came to be called a "simulcast" was the answer: that his style would be as good for television as for radio, and if he did both at the same time the matter of comparing his work with that of somebody else naturally would never arise.

Hugh Horler said later, "There actually wasn't as big a fuss about this as some people believed later, but naturally there was a lot of thought being given to it, that's all." Of course, while MacLaren's, Imperial Oil, the CBC, Conn Smythe and the other interested parties circled the issue warily, Horler had no doubts. He was on Foster's side all the way. Essentially, to the two of them, the rest was just fussing in the background.

Horler had worked with Foster for ten years then, and although they weren't close friends and didn't see one another except through hockey, they got along well. Horler did allow, however, that Foster was opinionated, "highly opinionated, not only about hockey, but about everything else. That didn't bother our relationship. I just rolled with it."

The clincher came in the spring of 1952. Famous Players, the movie company, had a mobile television unit, the only one in Canada. The Memorial Cup series for the Canadian junior championship was being played in the Gardens and MacLaren's obtained the Famous Players outfit for a closed-circuit televising of a game; Foster called it. The little screening room was crowded with observers. When the game was over, everyone was convinced. The battle had ended in style. There would be no need for Foster to change in any way. In that one test run, Foster proved he could call the game for both radio and television.

And so it came to pass that when the Leafs played their first game of the 1952–53 season, Foster came on the radio as usual with his ringing, "Hello, Canada!" and summarized the game to that point, then did the same half an hour later when the television cameras picked up the play.

Bud Turner has a little story about that game, the first ever shown on Canadian television. The CBC had named Sidney Newman, who had BBC experience, as producer. He later was to have many high-level jobs at the CBC and the National Film Board, but he hadn't quite mastered the inside attitudes of hockey.

"We were all up in the gondola, I remember," Turner said in 1985. "When the game was over Newman was ecstatic. 'This is going to be easy,' he said to Foster. 'It's just like ballet.' Foster and I exchanged a look I'll never forget. We knew we had a dilly."

Newman was replaced by Winnipegger George Retzlaff, as much a hockey bug as Horler and Hough. In a short time Retzlaff became a close, if ex-officio, member of the firm of Hewitt, Horler, Turner and Hough. His job was difficult in spots. The CBC had its own ways of doing things, one being a healthy resistance to abdicating too much control to sponsors and ad agencies. The key in this situation was Horler, who could always see the CBC's side as well as his own.

Of course, at the beginning there was a lot of experimentation. Camera positions were tried and discarded. A camera placed in the gondola made all the players look as if they were skating uphill. Placing cameras at mid-rink and at one end had a disorienting effect when the image being sent to air was switched from one camera to another.

The experimental nature of the whole first season was reflected in the fact that MacLaren paid only a hundred dollars a game for television rights that first year. They wanted to find out if they could handle it both artistically and commercially. And Conn Smythe went along with the low payment because he wasn't sure either. He wanted a full season to decide whether he liked television hockey enough to make it permanent.

Foster's input on the production side was considerable, especially when the debate included positioning of cameras. Smythe got into that, too. Bud Turner, involved in dealing with Smythe as well as with Imperial Oil, recalls that Smythe once insisted that in addition to one center-ice camera, another camera should be placed on the opposite side of the rink. When Turner pointed out the dizzying effect on viewers if the picture showed a player from one side, then switched to showing him from the other side, Smythe growled, "What's the matter with all the young men today, all they do is say no! I'm surrounded by people who say no! Doesn't anybody say yes any more?"

When television began, among the habits that disappeared was Foster's old system of walking in, chatting with a few people, warming up his voice toward airtime, then leaning toward the mike to begin addressing the multitudes. For television, crews began setting up in mid-afternoon, laying cables, hooking up the cameras, checking circuits, making sure the on-camera people were made up and that the lighting man had things under control in the intermission studio. Retzlaff's CBC crew of twelve would seem tiny today, but in contrast to radio it seemed like a mob.

Nothing less than television could have confirmed so

totally Foster's reputation for accuracy in calling hockey games. For all those years, going back to Ralph Allen's opinion that two hockey games were played in Toronto every Saturday night, the real game and the Hewitt game, there had been the feeling among skeptics that Foster might not be as good as he sounded.

"How do we know that when he says Ted Kennedy is forechecking hell out of the other guys, he's really doing anything but wave at them?" ran the discussions around tables loaded with ten-cent glasses of draft.

Now Foster had his chance, finally, to deal with those doubters, including those who claimed that his broadcasts were heavily dramatized.

Weekend Magazine commented waspishly, "The only difference is that now we can see Foster Hewitt's mistakes," but Foster wouldn't hold still for that kind of libel. "When people have a chance to both see and listen to the game, they realize that my comments are factual and instant," he retorted. "Also that my excitement is a natural outcome of what I am viewing and experiencing. Television, to me, instead of being an embarrassment, is actually a confirmation of my accurate reporting through the years."

At the same time Foster's voice was heard on two other projects. Both had their earliest outings during Leafs road games. One project was pay-TV, not to become a commercial reality for nearly thirty years. An experimental pay-TV system was set up in the Toronto suburb of Etobicoke. Customers got the games on cable and paid for each game they viewed. An adjunct was theatre television, games cabled in to nine theaters in Toronto and neighboring cities. The theatre project was based on the fact that home sets were few and far between at the time. But the costs were so high that audiences of five thousand or more would have been necessary to make them profitable. With the rapid increase of the number of home sets, the theatre showings were abandoned. The Etobicoke pay-TV circuit eventually disappeared as well.

Just a month after the 1952–53 hockey season opened, Foster suffered the most grievous blow of his life until that time. Station CKFH carried football games at that time, Bill calling play-by-play and Foster, from his long experience with Canadian football, handling the intermissions, including interviews.

On a Saturday, 15 November, they were at Varsity Stadium in Toronto covering a playoff game when a message from CKFH studios downtown brought shocking news. Police in Pennsylvania were trying urgently to get in touch with the Hewitt family. Foster's mother and father had been on a motor trip to the United States with their daughter Audrey and her husband, a Lever Brothers executive, Bert Massey. On one of those long Pennsylvania hills on a rainy, slippery day, Bert Massey had been driving uphill when an approaching vehicle skidded out of control.

Bert and Audrey were in the front seat. Foster's mother, Flora, was asleep in the back seat behind the driver. W.A. was awake, sitting on the other side of the back seat. Bert Massey wrenched the wheel to pull to the right, out of the way of the careening car, but didn't quite make it. The nose of his car got out of the way, but the other vehicle smashed in exactly where Flora Hewitt was having her nap. She was killed instantly. W.A. was bruised and battered, but survived.

That night Foster was to broadcast a Leafs game. There was no replacement available. Foster phoned the hospital where his father and the Masseys had been taken. Audrey, trying valiantly to hold herself together, told him how the accident had happened.

"I'll come," he said.

She said sadly that it wasn't necessary, she and Bert were all right, and could handle the arrangements. They'd be home in a day or so.

When the teams came to the ice that night at the Gardens, Foster was in the gondola broadcasting. The death of his mother was not mentioned on the broadcast and was not known to most listeners until the account of the accident appeared in the Toronto newspapers. The only time Foster wrote of the family tragedy was in a chapter about broadcasts that had been difficult because of pain or injury. Even this mention characteristically did not reveal Foster's inmost thoughts: "Never, of course, will I forget the broadcast on the night of the motorcar accident involving Mother and Dad, in which Mother was fatally injured. The distress on that occasion must forever be a personal memory."

12

HE FINALLY MISSES A GAME

●●●

"I was proud to be the voice that brought the games back home."
—Foster Hewitt talking about international hockey

ONE REASON FOSTER HEWITT DIDN'T MAKE CKFH'S MONday sales meetings was that for six or seven months of the year he wasn't home yet from the Sunday-night game. From the beginning he had had a full schedule. To that he first added a radio station and about two dozen employees. He had been just past his forty-eighth birthday when CKFH opened and he was always having to deny reports that he was in bad health. Now he had television, as well. Still, the work load never seemed to bother him.

Before Saturday games he would dine at home lightly and early, if at all. When a midweek game was on the agenda, he would work at CKFH until late afternoon, move to his Gardens office for whatever needed attention there, make his dressing-room visits and head for the gondola. If the Leafs were hitting the road for another city right after the game, he would park his overnight bag in his office and leave for the train straight from the Gardens. The trip might be a brief one for a Sunday-nighter in New York, Boston, Detroit or Chicago, but rarely in Montreal. Montreal had its own Saturday-night-home, Sunday-night-away tradition by then, with broadcasters covering the game separately in both French and English.

Of course, if the Leafs were going to be on the road for two games or more, Foster would be part of their travel plans. No NHL team traveled by air then (although when that did come to pass a few years later, Foster much preferred aircraft to the "always too hot or too cold" trains).

Foster's decision to broadcast every Leafs game, home and away, in those years after CKFH and television arrived wasn't, at least on the CKFH radio side, quite the bonanza that some people thought. But despite all the traveling with its resultant inconvenience and high expenses for line charges, the program did show a good profit. Davey's salesmen found hockey easy to sell. More important, CKFH's additions to the weekly menu for the Leafs' insatiable fans did more than anything to stake the station's claim in the hotly competitive Toronto market. Nobody else could carry the Leafs games, of course. As the Leafs' director of broadcasting, Foster had the say.

One of his main competitors was CKEY, then owned by Jack Kent Cooke—later of the Los Angeles Kings and Lakers, the Washington Redskins, owner of one of the continent's finest thoroughbred breeding establishments and a man who always hated being beaten at anything. At the time, Cooke owned the Toronto Maple Leafs of baseball's International League, so CKEY had the same kind of lock on baseball broadcasting Foster had on hockey. Foster was the first real challenge to Cooke's CKEY in the line of local sports coverage.

Which caused an incident involving Foster, who didn't like being beaten either. What happened was that CKEY, although it had no representative with the hockey Leafs on away games, began airing play-by-play reports by Joe Crysdale and Hal Kelly almost simultaneously with Foster's broadcasts. It seemed like a clear case of piracy, but obviously CKEY thought it was worth trying. It was not a new technique. Away back in the 1920s Foster himself once or twice had done what were called "reconstructed"

124

play-by-plays of other sports, the details telegraphed and then dramatized by Foster for broadcast.

But this was different. Foster was almost certain that CKEY was not getting its play-by-play information from any source other than his live broadcasts. But he couldn't easily prove it.

He discussed the matter with NHL president Clarence Campbell, who was also a lawyer, and decided to set a trap. In a broadcast from Boston he threw a few curves. He reported one player getting a penalty when he really hadn't, and he even threw in a spare goal when it wouldn't upset the game's result, just making a one-goal difference in the final score.

At the same time, someone back in Toronto taped the CKEY broadcast. Sure enough, the fake penalty and goal came across loud and clear in the voice of Joe Crysdale, CKEY's sports director. At the time, the Canadian Broadcasting Corporation was also the regulatory organization for all Canadian broadcasting. When Foster presented his proof of piracy, the CBC ruled that the reconstructions were illegal and ordered CKEY to desist. Problem solved.

Between games on the road, with the Leafs usually spending part of the day traveling, Foster would dine well in happy company. Hockey people have their favorite restaurants in every city and were generally, like Foster, traditionalists in the food line: roasts, steaks, chops in the inland cities; lobsters, crab and clams favored in Boston or New York. Foster might go out to eat with the Leafs' coach (Joe Primeau from 1950 to 1953, King Clancy and others after that). Other dinner companions included executives from other clubs or sports, local broadcasters or sports columnists and sometimes the regular hockey reporters for the three Toronto papers of the time, the *Star, Telegram* and *Globe and Mail*. They were all on expense accounts, so everyone paid his own way, which suited Foster.

On game days on the road he usually did not surface before noon and then ate lunch in his room. On a fine day he might go for a walk or do some shopping.

Otherwise he stayed in his room reading newspapers,

making a few phone calls, getting out of his pajamas only a couple of hours before game time. He'd call the game and then often have something quite hearty to eat. This meal might be on the run if the trip was for only one game with an overnight train to catch for home, which most players and coaches preferred. In that case he'd be back at his CKFH office soon after the train got in. So on he went in his single-minded pursuit of his career. Station CKFH needed that, Foster needed it and hockey could use it, too, moving into its finest era.

In those years approaching the middle 1950s, the Leafs had become a much different article from the exciting teams Foster had covered for the previous nearly thirty years. Five Stanley Cups (1945, 1947, 1948, 1949 and 1951) had been won under Conn Smythe's management with coaching by Hap Day and then Joe Primeau. King Clancy was unlucky enough to catch the Leafs on a downslide, one year not making the playoffs at all and two others getting knocked out in the first round. Maybe the losses and the lack of excitement helped Foster decide on a course that meant missing his first Leafs game in nearly thirty years—and also gave Bill his first major chance to show whether he deserved to be ranked as hockey broadcasting's crown prince.

In 1954 the Soviet Union, competing in the world hockey championships for the first time, hammered Canada 7–2 in the final game. True, the Canadian representatives had been the East York Lyndhursts—named for their sponsor, an auto dealership—who were no better than a slightly bolstered senior-B team. Still, senior-B teams and worse had won Olympic and world championships for Canada before. The first reaction in Canada was, what the hell happened? The second was an ultimatum to the poohbahs of Canadian amateur hockey: It better not happen again.

Because W.A. Hewitt had been one of the major forces in Canadian hockey all his adult life, Foster had more than the normal experience of international play. He had gone with W.A. to the Olympics at St. Moritz in 1928, back when to win Canada only had to show up. The

126

Soviets had changed all that. Canada determined to get even by sending the Allan Cup champion Penticton Vs to the 1955 championships in Krefeld, West Germany. The Vs, a strong team who softened their normal rough game in deference to the strict European referees, were in-and-outers in European exhibitions. When the world tournament began, and Canada's hockey constituency showed a feverish interest, Foster decided he'd better get over there for the final against the Soviets.

At first he saw the tournament only as an opportunity for CKFH to spend some of its own money to bolster its reputation as Canada's best hockey station. But Imperial Oil decided to get in, too, and arranged to sponsor the game on the CBC national radio network. What about the Leafs and his regular audience? Foster was asked. Foster told Bill this was his big chance, and to make the best of it.

For all his experience, Foster felt he had four-engined butterflies in his stomach when he approached the Krefeld rink. Canadian soldiers stationed in Europe and many Europeans as well had politicized the game tremendously. Foster experienced an excitement that he'd almost forgotten over the years. Strangers implored him to see that Canada won; "as if I could back-check or score."

The crowd at the rink was packed in so tightly that a puck shot over the boards had no chance whatever of falling to the floor. Even the catwalk behind the twenty-five radio booths was crowded, filled with noise in a dozen languages, none of them known to Foster. He thought of the millions at home waiting for his broadcast and wondered how many tens of millions around the world were waiting for all these broadcast voices to begin.

He luckily didn't know what happened in the instant the game did begin. One other Canadian broadcaster on hand was his old sparring partner from CKEY Joe Crysdale. Foster was supposed to have exclusive broadcast rights. But apparently Crysdale had bribed a German technician to rig up a telephone line for him; and he was all set to go when the puck was dropped.

By an incredible transmission error, what happened

when the game went on the air was that Foster's Canadian network got, "Hello, Canada, this is Joe Crysdale..." while CKEY listeners heard, "Hello, Canada, this is Foster Hewitt with your exclusive...."

But that switch in the phone lines was quickly repaired. In the end, with the anti-Soviet hullaballoo a constant roar in the background, Penticton won 5–0, even though for one stretch they played two men short.

Foster ranked what happened after the final whistle as one of the most emotional moments of his life. "When the game ended and Canadian servicemen leaped to the ice to hail their countrymen and the flags were paraded, I was so excited that my mouth went dry and I had to force my wrap-up comment." That hadn't happened for a while back home with the Leafs.

After that experience, Foster slotted Olympic and world championships into his schedules for years thereafter, not always without incident. He just wasn't his usual, efficient self abroad among all that patriotic excitement. He lost his admission card for the rink in Cortina at the 1956 Winter Olympics. The Italian doorman thought he was just another gate-crasher. Luckily, a United States sports columnist recognized him.

"Trouble, Mr. Hewitt?"

That brought an official and Foster got in—just in time to report the loss by Canada's Kitchener-Waterloo Dutchmen to the Soviets.

He covered the Whitby Dunlops' win at Oslo in the world championships of 1958, Belleville's win in Prague in 1959, and began to talk up, like other Canadians, the time when Canada's pros would be eligible to play the steadily improving Europeans.

13

ON THE ROAD AND AT HOME

● ● ●

"I got to be the advance man for Foster when
he'd go to help open television stations across
the country. One time we were in Kamloops in
the winter, very cold, and the radiators in this
motel were steaming and rattling, trying to
keep up with the frost outside. Foster went
into the bathroom for a shower—and suddenly
I heard this famous voice let out a wild scream,
wild hollering. He'd backed his bare ass into
the red-hot radiator."

—Bud Turner

IN THE DAYS WHEN TELEVISION STATIONS WERE SPREADING
across the land as fast as licenses could be obtained and
staff hired, it was the custom for the medium's stars to
cut the ribbon, bash a bottle of champagne against the
cornerstone, or whatever. Wayne and Shuster did it, the
stars of Front Page Challenge did it, singers and actors
and comedians were in much demand.

But no road show had exactly the style of Bud Turner
shepherding Foster Hewitt on his appointed rounds. In
Newfoundland, after the mayor of St. John's came out to
meet them and the major station-opening events there
were over, Turner and Foster drove from St. John's to

129

Corner Brook with a road map on the seat between them so they wouldn't miss a single Legion Hall or church basement along the way. The itinerary would be worked out, usually by Hugh Horler, to serve the purposes of the CBC and Imperial Oil, but Horler never went along. Turner was a willing guide, he says now, because he'd been born and raised in Toronto and was getting to parts of the country he'd never seen.

"That was the joy of it, not only to see the country but to see the way the country responded to Foster. Newfoundland, British Columbia, television stations, wherever we went he was wonderful. He'd go to open some service station, or celebrate a service station's tenth anniversary, any excuse to draw a crowd. He was the ideal guy for a sponsor to send out to a meeting of dealers or some other company function, incredibly loyal. Apart from those bigger events he'd go to some corner gas station and stand there by the pumps shaking hands and signing autographs, chatting, posing for pictures with some kid or old lady, it was all the same to him. It was show business and he was very good at it."

Ted Hough remembers being with Foster once in Detroit during a playoff between the Leafs and the Red Wings, back when no playoff was complete without one or both of those teams. Foster was crossing Woodward Avenue at noon hour, the wide street full of shoppers and lunch-goers. As they headed across, a policeman in the middle was directing traffic, waving briskly for right turns, left turns, straight-aheads, impatiently motioning the slower drivers to get a move on. When Foster reached the middle of the street, suddenly all activity stopped. The cop had recognized him and, taking a few steps, said, "Foster Hewitt!" They chatted for a minute. Then the cop fished an unused ticket from his pocket and said, "Would you sign this for me, please?"

Foster once remarked that, even in his radio-only days, it would have been almost impossible for him to escape from the scene of a crime if, in doing so, he had to speak to anybody. In Westminster Abbey once he happened to murmur a few words before a service began, and a man leaned

130

over from the row behind to say, "Aren't you Foster Hewitt?" That happened, with variations, everywhere he went—the Rossiya Hotel in Moscow, the rink at Stockholm, a hotel lobby in Rome; two whispering old ladies eyeing him in an elevator at the Savoy Hotel in London, a "Hello, Mr. Hewitt" at a beachfront restaurant in Nice. He never got used to it, never sought it, but enjoyed it when it did happen.

Yet the private Foster Hewitt had his moments, too. He had an eye for a good-looking woman. One, an ad-agency executive, remembers meeting him for the first time in New York after a game "and while I was still somewhat in awe, meeting this famous person, he said, 'Say, do you like dancing?' I said I did and he said, 'Great!' and took me dancing at the Copacabana, a really wonderful evening." In his thirties he didn't go along on some of the wildest nights out when the Toronto Maple Leafs were hockey's version of baseball's roistering St. Louis Cardinals and were known as hockey's Gashouse Gang. But later, perhaps when hotel rooms palled, he had been known to visit with others in the broadcast crew some of the infamous girlie clubs of Cicero, Illinois, where Chicago visitors went to see how the other half undressed.

One night when the lights went up on the strippers, another denizen of the place, looking around at his fellow art-lovers, was heard to cry, "That's Foster Hewitt over there!"

Many people, including his sister Audrey, describe him as having been a loner. But he also had to travel much of the time not only in the public eye but with groups of large and sometimes bruised, lacerated or bandaged gents who tended to draw the attention of passersby. If he had seemed standoffish the pro athletes would have been merciless in return. That never happened.

On most occasions, he was apparently more than willing to pitch in. In wartime when the NHL had to drop overtime so they could catch regularly scheduled trains to maintain schedules, the Leafs once missed their train to New York in a storm. Foster with them, they left Toronto by taxi to try to catch the train in Welland. At St. Catherines, faced with a pileup of stalled cars, Foster climbed out with the players and helped push the Leafs cabs around the cars. They missed the train at Welland anyway, then slipped and slid to Buffalo, getting there at 4:30 A.M. to find their first luck of the evening: the New York train was an hour late, so they caught it and got to New York in time for the game. One player described Foster as "one of the boys when things were going on, yet always just slightly removed, keeping his privacy."

His image was important to him. He would never have even one drink on the day of a game; he would not even walk through the Hot Stove Lounge at Maple Leaf Gardens on a game day in case somebody *thought* he'd been there for a drink. To him, there was a time for partying, but not when there was work to be done and an image to be preserved. He could hold his drinks, but knew that all he had to do was make one mistake in pronunciation when someone had smelled liquor on him and rumors would spread. Foster saw to it that the rumors never got a start.

An oddity is that one part of his public persona was, in some accounts, encouraged by Foster without regard for the reality. That was his famous frugality. Keith Davey used the word to mean what another jock, Leo Cahill, enshrined in his description of another frugal man as "a guy who throws nickels around like manhole covers." The story about Foster's check-dodging on overseas assignments started on his first one, when he traveled to Krefeld to cover the world hockey championships in 1955. Others on that trip said he always would join the gang for drinks but had an uncanny faculty of being able to require the bathroom just before the bill arrived. But to many others Foster was a man who never failed to pick up his share of any check. One of his later producers and traveling companions, Bob Gordon of MacLaren's, says it was embarrassing sometimes to have Foster always grabbing the check in restaurants. Ted Hough's version is that Foster was aware of his reputation, sometimes found it useful when he genuinely thought some expenditure or other was ex-

travagant and wasteful and used his penny-pinching reputation as a ploy "somewhat as Jack Benny used to do."

Foster apparently had decided from the beginning of
his career that whenever he was out on tour, he had no
responsibility for picking up checks in restaurants, bars,
wherever. Hugh Horler traveled with him only during
playoffs, but his memory is precise: "Foster never picked
up a check." On one of Foster's trips abroad to cover
world hockey, others in the CBC broadcast crew set him up
somehow by all agreeing to leave at once and stick him
with the bill.

Some of Foster's peculiarities, agreed to by everyone,
were so habitual that they became funny. One was this
matter of not picking up checks. Another was that there
was never any restaurant food anywhere that satisfied
him. The steaks were always too rare or too well done, or
whatever else was served was never quite right. It became
like a cartoon, a caricature, and when others would laugh
and kid him about it he'd laugh at himself.

One other side of Foster's character was a thinly veiled
prejudice against minorities. This attitude was undoubtedly a throwback to an old Toronto, the one he had grown
up in, the city that in Foster's early childhood discrimi-
nated openly in matters of race, color or religion. Nor was
such bigotry limited to Toronto. When Foster bought his
first summer property at Beaverton it was common to see
signs on lakefront communities stating "Gentiles Only."
Jews were unknown, or extremely rare, at Upper Canada
College. When the black and oriental population of Toronto began to grow, Foster's attitude (Bud Turner speaking) "offended me personally on many occasions. He was
highly prejudiced, awful, yet obviously he had some sense
of propriety in that what he said depended a lot on who
his audience was. He would never give a waiter or wait-
ress any difficulty, be unfailingly charming to everyone in
public and then he'd go back to his room and kick the
bedstead."

Like many prejudiced people, he made exceptions for
individuals, men or women he had come to know and like
personally. This was his version of, "Some of my best

133

friends are . . ." But other times he seemed reckless of consequences. Once, entering the Flame Showbar in Detroit after a hockey game, he stepped inside the door and exclaimed loudly enough for at least those nearby to hear, "Geez, the place is full of niggers!" There was an instant electricity in the air, but apparently it came to nothing or, more likely, Foster left.

In the 1970s there were public campaigns here and there against householders who had as lawn ornaments small plaster figures depicting a black jockey in racing silks. Foster had one on his lawn at Beaverton. Once when Ted Hough mentioned that it was offensive to some people, Foster replied, "There's no goddamn way I'm going to move that thing. That cost me two hundred dollars."

The propriety mentioned by Bud Turner obviously was in control most of the time. The only known public slip was one time when Foster said "Japs" on the air. For that one instant he must have had a flashback to the days when Japan was the enemy and headlines consistently used the term so offensive to the Japanese.

His relationships with Quebec broadcasters reflected a tendency to separate people by nationality. Bud Turner stated it bluntly: "You know, he hated the French." But, Quebeckers being able to look after themselves and in some cases harboring the same attitude in reverse, it was never a real problem. When Roland Saucier and the Quebec Hockey Night crew were working a playoff in French and Foster was doing it in English, they sometimes traveled together. Foster would tease them and they would tease him.

Turner recalls: "They knew exactly where he stood, that they were Frogs as far as he was concerned and wouldn't mind saying that to their face, practically. But in turn, and the reason they couldn't like him, was that he was so Anglo-Saxon, so English, that it was painful."

One story the French liked to tell on Foster was about an incident that took place in an aircraft flying to a hockey game. Foster was unhappy at being seated with one of the French crew. Also, he had been served a beef sandwich, tried it, and found it blah.

"I'd give a hundred dollars for some mustard," he grumbled aloud.

The Quebecker had just come back on an Air France flight from somewhere. Gleefully, but without a word, he reached into the breast pocket of his jacket, pulled out a plastic container of mustard and handed it to Foster. Touché, in spades. Foster looked amazed, muttered a cursory thanks, but didn't hand over the hundred dollars.

Hough had a concise explanation for Foster's lifelong aloofness from most of the normal roistering and other characteristic extramural activities of the sports world. "He was not a jock," Hough explained.

How could a man be Foster Hewitt, the voice of hockey, the connection whole generations had with the game, and be anything less than totally engrossed with sport? The answer was that while he could tell jock stories on the air, give audiences the feeling they were in the dressing room or wherever, he had many other interests that he couldn't share with full-time jocks.

Almost every summer he made an extended trip with a friend from his school days, Jim Grant, a businessman and investor, to look at mining properties, especially in western Canada, but also in the Caribbean and the Northwest Territories. Part of his understanding of the country came from those trips, including his habit of rounding off many of his summer trips with a stay at the Empress Hotel in Victoria. Jocks were as rare as whooping cranes in the lobby of the Empress where he and Grant took tea, which was served each afternoon among the potted palms to old parties listening to the music of Billy Tickle and his string quartet.

Hough tells of days off in Boston when he and Foster spent hours wandering in the graveyard a few minutes' walk from the old North Church, reading inscriptions on tombstones dating back two hundred years to the days of the American Revolution, and reflecting on life when those people were alive. In New York Foster habitually saw every hit musical that came along, from *Annie Get Your Gun* to *Guys and Dolls* to *Carousel* to *West Side Story*. He was so devoted to musicals that some of his friends expected that some time or other Foster would give regular airtime at CKFH to original cast recordings of famous Broadway musicals. Once when Foster had a day off in Boston he and Hough flew to New York solely to see the film *I Am Curious Yellow*, Foster kidding that he should be in some kind of a disguise in case somebody from North Battleford saw him buying a ticket to what was considered a gross sex film at that time.

For the world premiere of *Camelot* in Toronto, Foster bought a dozen excellent seats and invited friends to attend as his guests. He was always up on the latest movies and business-page stories, read a good deal and in other ways lived a life that he could separate from hockey.

Bill remembers him also as an ardent fisherman, first at Lake Simcoe, then at Camp Temagami, where both Foster and Bill had gone in their boyhood summers. The camp on Lake Temagami was owned by Foster's longtime friend and boxing tutor from Upper Canada College, A.L. Cochrane. The Hewitt cottage there bore a sign, "SeeKayFH." That was Kay's little joke, intended to mean that when visitors arrived it was to "See Kay and Foster Hewitt." No doubt she had been somewhat encouraged in this bit of work-connected whimsy by Foster's sign on the Beaverton place: "Genesso," for his first two major sponsors in hockey.

One of Bill's recollections:

> On fishing trips we'd go together to Temagami or to a place my first wife and I had at Lake Catchacoma. We'd get out in the boat and we'd really talk. We caught some good lake trout together in both places. When I was just a little guy, not even ten, there was an island of about five and a half acres for sale on Lake Temagami near the camp. Dad bought it and called it for me, Bill's Island. That was the place for when we really wanted to be alone: no electric light, no plumbing, a stove inside and a barbecue outside for cooking. We built a dock and had a good ax for cutting firewood.

Sometimes our talks when we were alone were about surface things, the fish, the day, the baits we used. Other times we'd talk about our lives. His and mine. There wasn't much about his life that he didn't have control of, but he was always interested in mine, what I thought, what I was doing, was my own family okay, was I happy. People used to say, I've heard them say it, that he was so preoccupied with his own life that he didn't have time for other things. That's crazy. He did have the faculty of shutting everything out if he had to. In the office maybe, you'd drop in with something to say and he'd be engrossed and he wouldn't even look up. He had total concentration. But then he'd look up and be with you. That concentration of his fooled a lot of people into thinking he didn't care. But I don't think anybody knew him better than I did, both as my father and my mentor and eventually my boss. He was the most generous man I ever met, and the most thoughtful about things that really counted.

Foster Hewitt was either very wise or incredibly lucky in winning Kay How as his wife. Maybe she was lucky, too—she said that from their earliest dates he was always comfortable to be with. As they settled into marriage, home and children, she obviously had no inclination to follow Foster on the normal mad dashes by taxi from rink to railroad station after a game. It just wasn't done, anyway. Wives never were along. The line in those days would have been, "It's no place for a woman." The rattlers heading for the border indeed were a male domain, with the players in a smoking room at one end of the car and everybody else in a smoking room at the other. It was standing room only at both ends in rooms that reeked of cigar smoke as the travelers ate sandwiches or had a drink or two before getting into their berths.

By all accounts, Kay had a happy, love-filled life, and managed their home as cheerfully and efficiently as Foster managed his career. She had, however, no interest in hockey whatsoever, and didn't care who knew it. At the two annual CKFH staff bashes, a golf tournament at Beaverton in the summer and the Christmas party at which Keith Davey was the regular Santa Claus for the staffers' kids, things sometimes got slightly uninhibited and the CKFH bunch would kid Kay that she didn't even *listen* to Foster's hockey broadcasts.

"I do so!" she would protest vehemently, but laughing. "I have to, so I'll be sure where he is."

Kay was a fine-looking woman. Her daughter Wendy said she was concerned about her weight but also that she carried it well. Keith Davey describes her as "gorgeous, handsome, fun to be with." June Callwood, writing for *Maclean's* in 1960 one of a series called "Famous Families At Home," found her "a woman with the innate graciousness that a background of wealth and affection often produces. . . . Kay Hewitt has never known hardship or argument; her face has a cloistered serenity and sweetness." And, later: "Convinced that a man's home should be a haven totally separated from his work, Kay has never in her life asked Foster how things are going at the office; in all their years he has never discussed a business concern with her."

Among those present at the Hewitt home in 1960 when Callwood visited was W.A. He was eighty-four and had lived with Foster and Kay since shortly after Flora Hewitt was fatally injured nearly eight years earlier. Callwood described W.A. as "a small, immaculate, chuckling, white-haired octogenarian who still works a full day in two Ontario Hockey Association offices, one at OHA headquarters and the other in Maple Leaf Gardens, where he is secretary. In the Hewitt tradition, Foster and Kay are delighted that he lives with them. The Hewitts all admire one another so much. . . .

"My conversation with the Hewitts turned on the affable axis of Foster's lack of pretension, Kay's mothering hospitality and the cheeriness of the elder Hewitt. . . .

Through it all ran the subject of hockey, the glittering, lurid and gawky sport that has dominated and been dominated by three generations of Hewitts."

One topic was Foster's resistance to illness, except on one occasion when he was covering the 1959 world hockey championships in Prague and developed pneumonia. He finally went to the all-important Soviet-Canada game with a temperature slightly over 104 and his eyes somewhat out of focus. " 'As soon as we heard his voice, Gramps and I knew he was very sick,' " interrupted Kay. 'Luckily we didn't know how bad it was.' "

When Foster landed by air in London soon after that game, his ears were bleeding from the flight pressure and he spent several days in the hospital.

At one point the conversation with Callwood turned to what was behind Foster's quiet, seemingly unemotional and untroubled manner. He admitted that he hated to lose but never lost his temper over losing, burning up inside instead; that sometimes he got depressed ("everyone has ups and downs"); that he was sensitive to criticism but "you just have to take it."

Callwood: "Whom do you confide in?"

Foster: "No one." Foster tapped his chest with a finger. "Myself."

His father nodded in amiable agreement. "Foster's always been like that," he said proudly.

One question that often cropped up in those days was Foster's appointment of Bill as manager of CKFH, which had happened a few years earlier.

Foster: "I've always feared the kind of criticism involved in that. When Bill moved in as manager he had two strikes against him, being the boss's son. I think he has overcome that because he is so good at his job. I don't see how

139

you can beat the problem. Why deprive him of an opportunity because you think someone will criticize you?"

One particularly telling passage came at the end of the Callwood article:

> Foster had observed earlier that his boyhood heroes had always been successful people. . . . He was asked now to define success.
> "I don't really know," he answered slowly. "I suppose no one really has it."
> "It's peace of mind," said Kay firmly.
> Foster considered this and shrugged. "I only know I'm happy in what I do."
> His father, almost dozing in a high-backed wing chair, roused himself. "That's success," he said gently. "Foster, that's success."

Socially, Foster was said by a friend, Waldo Holden of CFRB, to be simply not gregarious. "His idea of a good big party," Holden told writer Trent Frayne, "is about six people he's known for twenty years." The Hewitts sometimes had parties bigger than that, but only on major occasions, a landmark birthday or anniversary. Kay seemed to enjoy most the kind of informal gathering that had a lot of laughter in it, even if the laughter was at her or Foster's expense.

When the CKFH golf tournament ended each year, the guests and spouses, perhaps numbering forty or fifty, would gather at the lakeside house in Beaverton for drinks from a well-stocked bar. Foster spared no expense. There would be games, including horseshoe pitching, followed by a lavish barbecue. It was usually Keith Davey's job to thank the Hewitts for the party. Once he ended his speech with sort of a character sketch of Foster, concluding with these lines:

140

So send the bum off to an island
With a gallon of Esso crammed down his pink
   throat
And here's to the Leafs
May they always be plastered
And the same to Foster,
That marvelous bastard.

Foster and Kay, Davey thought at the time, were vastly amused. Bill was rather shocked; he admired his father so much that barbed kidding tended to make him uneasy.

Foster's sense of humor was keen, sometimes even zany. But there were limits, demonstrated when another of Davey's sallies didn't work out so well. Frank Somerville, Ann's husband, was for a time on the sales force at CKFH. Davey described him as a "taciturn kind of a lazy, droll guy, but a very, very nice guy. One day we're sitting in the sales meeting in Foster's office on the second floor at Grenville Street and we look out of the window and all of a sudden there's a whole bunch of ladders and firemen going up to the roof of the building.

"There was an instant of surprise and then Somerville said, 'Quick, somebody phone CHUM and find out what's happening.'

"It was a very comical statement, I thought terribly funny, and knowing Foster to have such a good sense of humor, I told him."

It was one of Davey's bad guesses. "Foster was just furious with Somerville and furious with everybody." Bill mentioned later that his brother-in-law didn't work at the station for very long.

Politically, Foster was what Davey called "a closet Tory." Through Davey's own Liberal connections at the time he often heard that the Tories were after Foster to run for office, but Foster would just laugh that off.

Meanwhile, Davey was becoming more and more active in the Liberal Party. A couple of times he was offered political posts, but Foster always managed to talk him out of leaving, thus postponing Davey's move into what eventually was to become *the* major behind-the-scenes political career of the 1960s and 1970s.

In the early 1960s, with the Liberals out of power in Ottawa, a small group in Toronto, calling itself Cell-13, met every Wednesday night for dinner. They included Davey; Walter Gordon, soon to become finance minister; Dan Lang and Royce Frith, eventually to become senators (as did Davey); and David Anderson, a senior Toronto Liberal. One week they had a crisis. The party's national director had fallen off the wagon with a resounding crash and a replacement was urgently needed. Within a day, the job had been offered to Davey and he decided to take it, a move that changed the direction of his life.

He made that decision just before the 1961 Stanley Cup playoffs, but didn't want to resign just as Foster was facing his heaviest schedule of the year. But as soon as the playoffs were over, he went in to Foster's office, gazed over the top of the little toy royal carriage and horses sitting on Foster's desk and said, "Foster, I've made a decision. It's absolutely irrevocable so there's no point in us discussing it at any length."

Foster didn't have to be told. He looked up. "You're going to leave and go into politics."

"Yes, I am."

Foster threw a dinner for Davey at the Granite Club with a lot of key people in the radio business present. He gave Davey a big reclining chair and bade him a fond farewell.

14

CHANGES AT THE GARDENS, TRAGEDY AT HOME

● ● ●

"It did feel a little strange, sitting beside Bill the first night he took over the television. I'd thought I was prepared for it. Bill said it felt strange to him, too."
—Foster Hewitt, in 1957

BILL HEWITT KNEW THAT HIS CHANCE TO MOVE INTO HOCKEY Night in Canada full-time depended, in a sense, on Foster. If Foster didn't vacate the mike, nobody was going to push him away from it. Maybe it was typical that when Foster gave Bill his chance it was done obliquely, as a necessary corollary to his decision to cover the world championships at Krefeld in 1955.

Bill recalls: "That was my break and he made it for me. He just said to me very casually, 'Now, I'm going over there and you're in charge. You look after the television and your mother.' Then he laughed and added, 'And I won't worry about anything.' We talked about it some more and he said if there was ever an opportunity for the public to accept me, this was it, for me to make it or break it."

Bill was ready. As sports director at CKFH (his appointment as station manager came a little after Krefeld, when Howard Caine, the original manager, applied for

143

and received his own broadcasting license as CHWO Oakville), Bill had been covering every sport in the city. Junior hockey was his specialty, and he already knew many
players in the NHL. He also had confidence enough to want
his father to stand aside and let the young guy at it. Some
people thought Foster something of a tyrant in the way he
gave Bill advice loud and clear, but Bill apparently never
minded—he'd started listening to his father's advice on
broadcasting long, long ago.

So when he did his first simulcast in the spring of
1955 Bill's style had been honed in those long years at
Foster's side to the extent that, as Foster said, "some
people hardly noticed the difference."

On his return from Krefeld, Foster went back to the
telecasts for two years. Then he officially turned the play-
by-play over to Bill. For another year Foster stayed on
television as color commentator and also announced the
three stars at game's end. He continued to do the road
games on radio, and from 1958 concentrated almost entirely on radio. For some years before that, the Leafs had
been no bargain to cover for anyone who had known them
in their heyday. Howie Meeker had followed Clancy as
coach, and Billy Reay had followed Meeker, but in those
two years the Leafs had finished fifth once and last once.
To most Canadians, no playoffs and no Foster in the spring
was like no robins.

Conn Smythe was unhappy. He called his players a
bunch of jellyfish and, being beyond his own sixtieth birthday, began looking for ways to get out of hockey. His idea
was to start a youth movement among the Gardens directors, organize them as the hockey committee with his son
Stafford as chairman, provide a budget so some of them
could travel with the team and eventually pass his control
to Stafford.

The main personalities among the mainly blue-blood
assortment of young Toronto sports, all successful in their
own varied careers, were Stafford, Toronto *Telegram* publisher John Bassett, and the not-yet-famous Harold Ballard.
Stafford and Ballard had been cronies for years in the
management of the Leafs' junior farm team, the Marl-

boros, a club started more than thirty years earlier by the senior Frank Selke.

Stafford made the move that was to turn the Leafs' fortune around. One of the most successful minor-league executives in 1958 was George (Punch) Imlach. Stafford talked to him at the NHL meetings in Montreal, and eventually, after some tough negotiating in Toronto, they made a deal. Imlach even then wanted more control than Stafford was willing to give, a battle that Imlach eventually won. But the real Imlach era arrived when, two months into his first season and with the Leafs still not going anywhere, Imlach fired Billy Reay and took over the coaching himself.

Foster and Imlach made quite a pair. Foster had known of Imlach in the 1930s when Punch played junior and senior hockey around Toronto. Imlach remembers: "He always used to call me George Gimlick then." To Imlach, Foster was a legend of his youth, but they became friends on quite a different basis: they had fun together on the road. It's doubtful that Foster ever met anyone who razzed him the way Imlach did. Foster, instead of getting his back up, seemed to enjoy it.

When he picked the three stars of a game, it didn't matter who they were or how well-founded his choices, there were always some dissenters, especially among the combatants themselves. Imlach used this. When Foster would walk into the team's special sleeping car (or later a chartered aircraft), Imlach would have the jokers on his team primed.

As soon as Foster got aboard and settled, Imlach would get up and say loudly, "Foster, those three stars—for cripes' sake, what game were you broadcasting? How could you pick those guys?"

Other Leafs would take up the chorus and Foster would scrunch down in his seat, growling but sort of enjoying it. Somebody like Allan Stanley or Tim Horton might kid him a bit later about the razzing and Foster would just grumble, "That Imlach!" and laugh, becoming more human to those Leafs because they knew he could take the kidding, like the rest of them.

145

Imlach said he enjoyed Foster's company, and Foster seemed to enjoy his, but it was mainly what Imlach called "more being sociable than being close friends." To describe their relationship as much more than that probably would be an exaggeration. Foster went home after some of their early outings and told his family that he really liked Imlach. It was because of Foster's way of life that, as in many of his other hockey friendships, they weren't often in each other's company away from hockey.

No doubt part of the bond between them came because Foster, missing the excitement that attended the Leafs in their best years and regretting the lack of it through most of the 1950s, found the convivial, controversial Imlach a personal tonic as well as a broadcaster's bonanza. All through the 1958–59 season the Leafs were in last place, with Imlach always telling whoever would listen that they were going to rise up and make the Stanley Cup playoffs. Which they did.

You can imagine Foster's growing excitement as he called the season's last five games—two weeks of remarkable suspense. On 9 March the Leafs were last, nine points out of the fourth and the last playoff spot. On 22 March, having beaten Boston, the New York Rangers, Montreal and Chicago, they were fifth, one point from fourth. On the final night in Detroit, Foster's voice rang out of the radio as it hadn't for years . . . the Cinderella Leafs this and the Cinderella Leafs that. They were down 2–0, then went ahead but were tied 4–4 going into the third. Dick Duff got the winner from Larry Regan, and Billy Harris scored again, to make it 6–4. The Leafs got past Boston that year in the semifinal before losing to Montreal in the final. Obviously they were on their way.

From then on Foster and Imlach traveled a lot of miles together, and not only to and from games. In New York, the Leafs stayed at the Commodore, a few blocks from a Third Avenue bar called the Old Seidelburg. The bar's now gone but in those days it was a mecca for devotees of German food and beer. The team would check in, then Imlach would get on the phone and organize the rest-and-recreation party, which as a matter of Imlach's

146

policy never included the players, who had their own places to go.

"Mr. Hewitt!"

"Mr. Imlach!"

"Meet us in the lobby in five minutes or we'll leave you behind."

Often Foster would pass. "Mostly he'd just go to bed," Imlach said. "He was, well, kind of quiet. Minded his own business pretty well. But we'd always ask him and when he came with the gang he was a hell of a guy."

Foster's normal drink was rye and ginger ale. If he wanted something heavier, he'd have a Manhattan, also made with rye. Vodka Gibsons were another favorite. But on the nights when he and Imlach tramped down Third Avenue talking about last night's game or hockey in general or whatever, usually with a hockey writer or two along, they never had to discuss what they were going to have at the Old Seidelburg. The place would be full of printers from nearby newspapers, New York reporters and other strays. A few would call out to Foster and Imlach, recognizing them from previous visits.

Imlach would order: "Dark Kulmbacher all around." The bartender would start drawing beer into big white crockery steins, looking over the pull handle to enquire, "And?"

"And," Imlach would say, with Foster groaning behind him that his stomach couldn't stand it, "a plate of Leiderkranz cheese and Spanish-onion sandwiches on pumpernickel."

Imlach claimed that this combination was his secret weapon in New York—that all he had to do was breathe on Ranger players going by and they'd slow right down. A couple of hours of decompression later they'd go back to the Commodore to bed, except on those not especially rare occasions when they decided to carry on down to Greenwich Village and listen to some music.

The new spirit that Imlach brought to the Leafs, including the push he inspired them to make from last place to the playoffs in the final two weeks of his first season, undoubtedly was part of what made Foster a pretty good night owl in those days.

Imlach had a special nickname for Foster: "Chickie." Few knew the origin. It dated from a time when the Leafs missed their normal transportation and wound up driving to Buffalo to catch a train. There was an hour to wait and Foster and the others were hungry and tired. They went to a restaurant called Chickie's, which had just closed. Imlach led Foster around the back, and through the kitchen door, asking, "Whattaya got to eat?"

They'd often eaten chicken, the restaurant's specialty, there. But when Foster saw the revolting state the kitchen was in, only his hunger and the fact that no other place was open kept him from bolting. Finally he ordered an omelet, groaning, "There's nothing much they can do wrong to eggs." Nobody felt sorry for him; he'd done too much complaining about first-rate meals to get any sympathy. After that when Imlach called him Chickie, Foster would groan and remember.

Conn Smythe sold his Gardens shares to his son Stafford in 1961. Stafford in turn brought in John Bassett and Harold Ballard as partners in the bank loan they had to get for the share purchase. Bassett was the largest shareholder and, besides being the proprietor of his *Telegram* newspaper, was principal owner of the city's first private television station, CFTO. Foster's name had been among those on the license application for what was considered to be potentially the richest television prize in the country.

Bassett's recollection shows Foster as a tough, conservative businessman playing for very high stakes:

> We knew one another, but not very well. When I put the company together, Baton Broadcasting, Foster came to me and said he would like to get in for ten percent, and that he felt he had a standing that would help the license application. I said, "Sure, you're welcome, you'll

become a member of the board. Just send your money around."

Then we were together a great deal working on the application and I got to know him better—his advice was always good. In Baton the Telegram Corporation, which actually owned the stock, had fifty-one percent. The next-biggest shareholder was a company called Aldred-Rogers, for Joel Aldred and Ted Rogers. I became chairman. Aldred wanted to be president and that was all right with me because at the *Telegram* I was in a life-and-death battle with the *Star* that needed all my attention.

Then Foster told me he was concerned, felt that Aldred was being very extravagant at CFTO. Well, I supported Aldred at first, but not for long—we were losing a pile of money. Three months after we went on the air [New Year's Day, 1961], it was plain that it just wasn't working out. I told Aldred that and we discussed quite amicably what should be done. In the end I bought him out and became president, but then there was a lot of cleaning up to do. That's where Foster, with his eye for the buck, came in. He was helping us, very helpful, and one of the most helpful things he did was suggest a man he knew, Bill Crampton, to come in as general manager. He had a lot of dirty work to do, fired about two hundred people, helped turn things around—and he'd been Foster's idea. Foster and I became very close through this whole operation, became greater friends, went through a lot together, paid off our debts and in the end it made him about twenty-five million dollars. Somewhere in there he was made a vice-president of CFTO and many of our other companies, which he was for life.

How about socially?

But they didn't socialize. "I was never in his house and he was never in mine."

Back at the Gardens, while this was going on, Stafford and Ballard seemed to get along with Bassett all right, but there was one main difference among them. While Foster and Bassett had become good friends, the other two tended to run Foster down. This was an attitude he'd never had to face in the Gardens before. When some offices were being renovated, Foster—who had been there for more than thirty years—found his was eliminated.

"It was my experience," Imlach said, "being there in the middle of it, that Stafford and Ballard never appreciated Foster. All that he had done, of course, was do more than any other one man to build the franchise into a gold mine for them, or anyone else, to own."

Foster undoubtedly noticed the occasional slurs, but he ignored them. He'd known Stafford from boyhood, and Ballard was a Hewitt family friend going back to the 1928 Olympics, when Ballard had been W.A.'s assistant manager of the Canadian hockey gold medalists. Foster had outlasted a lot of people around the Gardens and he seemed willing to take his chances this time. Instead of responding, he simply concentrated on his job.

He was also having fun again. During the Imlach sixties Foster was in his best form. He had a real old-time Leafs team to cover again, with characters that rivaled his favorites of the 1930s: Frank Mahovlich, Bob Pulford, Dave Keon, Johnny Bower, Red Kelly, Billy Harris, Tim Horton, Allan Stanley, Bert Olmstead, Dick Duff, Bob Baun, Carl Brewer, George Armstrong and others. Leafs were always at the top or near it and won Stanley Cups in 1962, 1963, and 1964. As for the rest of the league, the Rocket was gone but Gordie Howe was still in Detroit, Bobby Hull and Stan Mikita in Chicago, Jean Beliveau and Dickie Moore in Montreal. Andy Bathgate came from New York to join the Leafs for their 1964 Stanley Cup. It was all hockey as Foster had known it, hard and sometimes dirty, but there were players to conjure with from a broadcast booth.

By that time, Foster had a new traveling companion on Sunday-night and midweek radio trips. Bob Gordon of MacLaren Advertising was no stranger to Foster when they began traveling regularly together in the middle sixties. As a junior at the agency in 1959, Gordon's first trip with Foster had been memorable: it was on 23 March, the morning after the last night of that season when the Leafs beat Detroit and made the playoffs by a single point.

After the game, the team's air charter, a mode of travel unusual for them at the time, touched down briefly in Toronto to let off Foster and a few others. Then Imlach and his Cinderella team flew on to Boston.

Foster knew what he was doing, getting off in Toronto: he was guarding the resting-up time he knew he would need as long as the Leafs survived in the playoffs. He could see in his mind the aircraft landing in Boston, the player bus stopping at the Boston Garden to unload equipment, reaching the Copley Plaza Hotel at maybe 4:00 A.M., Imlach and others getting to bed eventually but by no means immediately.

So, after a good night's sleep, Foster was on hand the following day when the main broadcast crews, Bob Gordon among them, loaded up for Boston. Gordon was a fairly typical young Canadian hockey fan of his time. He'd first seen Foster at the hockey studio at Maple Leaf Gardens. He remembered years later: "I saw him come in and I thought, My God, that's Foster Hewitt! I just couldn't believe that I was in the same room with him."

They hadn't, however, met often, Gordon being a radio operator for others at the time, but he'd been assigned to the Boston trip. Gordon has never forgotten that first ride to Boston:

"I can't remember details of the flight much except I knew I was safe. The plane wouldn't crash with Foster Hewitt on it. Ted Hough was there, too, of course, and the Hot Stove League people, Jack Dennett and Wes McKnight. When we landed it was the first time I had really seen Foster in action. First thing we had to do, straight off the airplane, was go to a place called Seafood Harbor House, which was like a great big warehouse. I'd never eaten a clam in my life. Foster went through four buckets of steamed clams, just like that, dozens and dozens of them."

Bob Gordon was to find later, in ten years or more of traveling with Foster, covering every Leafs out-of-town game, that Foster had a system for every city in the old league: Boston, New York, Chicago, Montreal and Detroit; then, with NHL expansion: Pittsburgh, Los Angeles, Philadelphia, Minnesota, St. Louis, Oakland; Buffalo and Vancouver, Atlanta and Long Island. If there was any place open for food and drink when they got in, they'd go straight to it, then to the hotel to rest, sleep, relax until game time. After the game the charter would usually take them home again, landing in Toronto well after midnight. Foster was well into his sixties by then, but showing no signs of wanting to slow down.

Even though they were together constantly, they rarely delved deeply into one another's lives. Perhaps the age difference played a part, perhaps Foster's sense of privacy. Gordon remembers him speaking often of W.A., who by the middle 1960s required constant care and had moved happily to an institution not far from the Hewitt home. Bill Hewitt, also very close to his grandfather, said, "Dad visited him there every blessed day that Dad was in town, and phoned him every day when he was on the road, until grandfather died one night in his sleep." That was in September 1966, a few months past W.A.'s ninety-first birthday. Ted Hough recalls, "I helped Foster clean out the closet at Rosemary Road where all his father's things were, finding the suit that Foster was to take to the undertaker and so on. We were going through all of W.A.'s old ties, wide, wide ties, and I kept saying to Foster, 'Let's be ruthless and throw these things out.' Foster would look at the ties and say, 'No, I'll be able to use these, the style is going to come back.' "

But an exception in Foster keeping his private life to himself came a couple of years later. At that time Kay Hewitt had been ill for a few months, suffering pain and nausea. Eventually her doctor ordered her to stay in the hospital for a complete examination. On the day Kay was to have exploratory surgery, Foster and Gordon were on their way to Chicago.

On the team bus they sat together. That night, driving away from the old LaSalle Hotel where the Leafs stayed then, Gordon thought Foster was unusually quiet. Normally on that ride from hotel to rink through the rough districts of Chicago, he'd look out the windows at ruined neighborhoods, fights going on, and comment: "Hey, look at that! Look over there." That night he didn't say anything.

Gordon finally asked, "Foster, you okay?"

Foster said, "No, not really. I just got the word on Kathleen. Bill phoned to say I was to call the doctor and he told me it's cancer. They operated and found there was nothing they could do. The doctor told me she doesn't have long to live." Then he talked quietly for a while about how much his wife meant to him and to the whole family.

Gordon didn't know quite how to respond, but at one point asked Foster if he wanted to skip the game.

"Oh, no, no," Foster said.

Gordon thought Foster had confided in Punch Imlach, as well. But what he remembered most clearly about that night was walking behind Foster up the long steps to the broadcast position. Foster usually hurried up those steps, eager, looking around, taking it all in. This time his head stayed down all the way.

Once he was in place, the mike in front of him, he seemed to put his sorrow out of mind, and called the game as usual, the complete pro. As soon as it was over he fell quiet again and kept to himself on the ride home.

For months afterward the home on Rosemary Road was a sad place. The decisions to be made were difficult and yet predictable. The only thing that could be done for Kay was to make her last months as comfortable as possible, and one way to do that was to have life's routines go on as if she was going to live forever. Foster spent more and more time at home, spelled off frequently by Wendy and Ann. Bill and his family lived not far away so when the weekend games came and Foster left with the team

153

late Saturday, Bill would leave his own family (wife, son and three daughters) to stay with his mother, sharing again the same closeness they'd had from when he was a child.

In the end, home care was no longer possible. Kay died in hospital, her family around her, late in January 1969, and was buried in the family plot in Mount Pleasant Cemetery in the north midtown area of Toronto.

15

A BIG GOAL—
AND A
RISK-FREE PROFIT

● ● ●

"He was the best, absolutely."
—Don Cherry, hockey analyst

IT MAY STRIKE THE READER THAT A LOT HAS BEEN SAID ABOUT
Foster as a peerless hockey broadcaster without producing
any but circumstantial evidence. Many will have heard
hundreds of Foster's broadcasts, but few would have had
the opportunity to read transcripts of his tapes. For that
reason one particular goal from a variety of possibilities is
offered here.

First, an introduction. By the spring of 1967 Foster
had seen Punch Imlach's Leafs in operation for nine years.
He had seen Imlach promptly, openly, directly, and occasionally rudely, defend his prerogatives against all comers,
including the team owners. Some players might not have
liked him but they certainly recognized that whatever it
was he was doing was putting playoff money in their bank
accounts year after year. Then, even the top players could
use a little extra money from time to time.) By 1967 the
Leafs were getting a little long in the tooth but they still
made it to the final against an excellent Montreal team,
which, with the addition in the 1964–65 season of Leafs
fine money player Dick Duff, had won Stanley Cups for
the past two years. They were also to win the next two.

But this was 1967 and Imlach's old lions had a few roars left.

Montreal won the opening game of the series 6–2 ("a cakewalk," Foster called it, naturally). But by the time the last two minutes were ticking away in the sixth game, on 2 May in Toronto, the Leafs were ahead in the series three games to two and led the game 2–1.

Bill Hewitt was calling the game for television, Foster for radio. This transcript of Foster's voice begins less than two minutes from the end of the game. Some, for old times' sake, can be forgiven for reading it aloud:

The crowd can hardly contain themselves during this dramatic struggle. It has been a terrific game all the way. Now someone has thrown what appears to be an egg midway between the Canadiens' blueline and their goal, and the scrapers are coming out. It is rather unusual for any object to be thrown on Gardens ice, but the delay may be a great help to both sides because all players seem to be almost exhausted.

Leafs have outscored Montreal but the latter have been putting on a terrific drive during this third period, with the Toronto team desperately countering every attack.

Beliveau has been the Montreal leader while Davey Keon has been here, there and everywhere. Both Worsley and Sawchuk have been outstanding; the latter truly sensational.

The ice clearing has finished and the teams are ready for the face-off in the Montreal area. The puck slides to the boards. Armstrong has a whack at it. Laperriere carries it back of the net. It slides off his stick and rolls to center ice. Pronovost picks it up and shoots it back into the corner. Leafs seem intent on keeping the puck in Canadiens' defensive zone. Duff carries the puck out to center ice, where he is again checked by Pronovost, who retained it for a few seconds and then fired it once more toward the Montreal goal. J.C. Tremblay stickhandles around his own net and feeds the puck to speedy Cournoyer. But he is blocked by Hillman and the puck is again shot into the Canadiens' corner. Every Montreal attack is frustrated by a stubborn Toronto defence, determined to prevent even a shot at their own goal.

There are only fifty-five seconds of regulation time remaining. Toronto leads two goals to one. The hometown crowd is anticipating a Stanley Cup victory, while Montreal Canadiens are using every strategy to get the tying goal and push the result into overtime.

With less than a minute remaining, Leafs are called for icing and the referee calls for a face-off to the left of Leafs' goal. There's a delay in play and Montreal goalkeeper Gump Worsley doesn't know whether or not coach Toe Blake wants him to come out of the net.

Now Blake has decided to remove Worsley. He's going to the bench. With fifty-five seconds to play, Montreal will use six attackers and their goal is empty. Canadiens intend to shoot the works. Beliveau is coming on the ice. So are Roberts, Cournoyer, Ferguson, Richard and Laperriere. It's all or nothing for them now.

Leafs, too, are making changes. Imlach is making his stand with an all-veteran lineup of Stanley, Horton, Kelly, Pulford and Armstrong. Sawchuk, of course, is in goal. Beliveau will face off for Montreal and Stanley for Toronto. Armstrong is still at the bench talking to coach Imlach. Referee John Ashley is becoming impatient. Ferguson skates over to talk to Beliveau. Stanley is hesitating; now he comes into position. This face-off is vital. They're all set.

The puck is dropped. Stanley gets possession. He snaps the puck to Kelly. Kelly kicks it to Pulford. Pulford passes to Armstrong. Armstrong is driving hard! Army shoots toward the empty net! It's on target . . . *It's in! He scores!* Armstrong has scored the insurance goal. It's now Leafs three, Canadiens one. Toe Blake's strategy backfired and that shot has just about decided possession of the Stanley Cup. Canadiens had to gamble everything but lost. Time of the goal, nineteen twenty-three. Only forty-seven seconds from the end of the game.

Worsley returned to the Montreal net and play resumed and continued through forty routine seconds. Then, picking up Foster again for the game's climax:

"Seven seconds! Six, five, four, three, two, one! The game is over! Leafs have won the Stanley Cup. The Toronto players are mobbing each other. The crowd is wild. There's no use trying to talk against that uproar. The final score is Leafs three, Canadiens one. By their well-earned victory Toronto Maple Leafs are Stanley Cup champions for 1966–67, their fourth triumph in six years. A truly great record."

That was the last game played in the old six-team league. It is also the last time the Leafs won the Stanley Cup. And while it was not seen at the time as the beginning of Foster's exit from the profession he had ruled forever, it seemed, he would be part of the absolute heights of the game only once again—in Moscow in 1972.

Foster's shrewdness about money is not as easy to delineate as his broadcasting skill. He simply seemed to be very good at spotting projects that would make money but that were not too much of a gamble. Unlike those who may parlay a series of stock-market tips into quick profits and by doing so amass a quick fortune, Foster had a credo: "If it's worth buying, it's worth keeping." His long-term investment in Madsen Red Lake Mines was the cornerstone of a portfolio that eventually made him a solidly based multimillionaire. He believed in the group John Bassett put together to seek approval for Toronto's CFTO-TV, so he invested in what became Toronto's second television station and the country's richest, the first competition for the CBC in the Toronto market. There is no doubt, of course, that Foster's name on the application, along with John Bassett's and the other principals, was a strong factor in the license's being granted.

Another investment didn't return profits in the millions as his original CFTO-TV stock did, but was an example of Foster's belief that the best way to pursue a buck was to have someone guarantee that you can't lose. In that case, the worst that can happen is you break even. Or you might double the money you didn't have to spend in the first place.

This investment involved the Vancouver Canucks hockey club in the late 1960s. It was then a minor-league franchise, but Vancouver was seen by many as a city with major-league potential. There had been cries of rage and pain in Canada when NHL expansion in 1967, from six teams to twelve took in six United States teams and turned down Vancouver. It was pretty well accepted that Vancouver would be a sure thing in the next expansion, due in 1970, and the minor-league franchise probably would become the vehicle for the jump to the big time. So for anyone who wanted to become an NHL club owner, buying into the Canucks right then was attractive.

There are always wheels within wheels. In Vancouver there was a shrewd feeling that it wouldn't hurt to have a surefire big-league general manager among the eventual applicants. In 1967, Punch Imlach's Leafs had just won their fourth Stanley Cup in six years, and Imlach was generally rated with Sam Pollock of Montreal as the greatest hockey genius on the planet. So someone phoned Imlach from Vancouver and made an offer, thirteen percent of the Canucks for fifty-five thousand dollars. Apparently, the club ownership was being divided into seven equal units, each shareholder having the right to pay an equivalent share of the NHL new franchise fee (which had been two million dollars per club in 1967) when the time came.

Imlach's caller said, "Do you think Foster would come in?"

It was a possibility, Imlach said, but he didn't really know.

The Vancouver contact then phoned Foster and repeated the proposition. A few days later, when Imlach and Foster happened to meet, Vancouver was mentioned and Punch said, "You going in?"

Foster: "Yeah. I think it's a good idea."

Imlach did, too, so that was it.

Imlach, being under contract to the Leafs, registered his shares in the name of a British Columbia executive. Foster's were in his own name. Now comes the funny part, if this is the kind of thing that amuses you.

In those days, MacLaren's had contracts to produce hockey broadcasts in the NHL's two Canadian cities, Toronto and Montreal. Hockey Night in Canada had become by then a prime commercial property, always topping the program ratings, with studios and film crews and play-by-play announcers in both French and English, all in all a massive operation. And the thought of someone else grabbing all those rights to a Vancouver franchise caused some stony stares into the bottoms of Gibson glasses.

MacLaren's definitely wanted to have an ownership position in the new franchise, so that they could have a say in the disposal of rights. But for some reason that isn't clear now (today sponsors routinely buy baseball and hockey teams to gain long-term exclusivity in commercial exploitation), MacLaren's didn't think it should buy into Vancouver under its own name.

So MacLaren's approached Foster. Whether this was before or after Vancouver had contacted him is uncertain. What is certain is that while Imlach put up his own money, MacLaren's either put up or otherwise guaranteed the amount Foster would need. Foster just lent MacLaren's his name. Two years later when the franchise was granted, however, the entry fee was to be six million dollars, instead of the two million Imlach had been figuring on. His share of the six-million-dollar purchase price would have been nearly nine hundred thousand dollars, and he didn't want to go in hock to the bank for that much. He sold out to the successful applicants, a company called Medicor from Minneapolis, for a substantial profit. Foster did the same. His big advantage was that although he hadn't been playing with his own money, nobody had thought to write out what would happen if the deal turned a profit. As everything else had been secret except to three or four insiders (even Imlach did not know that MacLaren's had backed Foster), the profit belonged to Foster. One estimate is about half a million dollars, which might be just a shade high.

It still rankled Foster and Imlach a little in subsequent years, the way that franchise was sold. Medicor was offered a time-payment plan rather than the original lump-sum demand that Imlach had balked at. Time payments could have been handled by Hewitt, Imlach and company. Also, turning down a group headed by two of hockey's greatest names in favor of some carpetbaggers from the United States seemed shockingly out of sync with sanity.

Which later events proved rather dramatically to be true. The head of Medicor and of the new NHL franchise was convicted a few years later on charges of illegally moving assets from the Canadian company to one of Medicor's United States subsidiaries. The Vancouver club subsequently changed ownership, and the team suffered from lack of steady direction.

As Imlach said in 1985, "One thing for damn sure, Vancouver would have had a much different hockey experience in the last fifteen years if they'd started out with Foster Hewitt and me among the owners."

16

BATTLE OF THE GARDENS

● ● ●

"Harold Ballard never forgave Foster for turning his back on him over those charges that sent Ballard to jail. Foster never forgave Harold for what has happened to the Leafs since then."

—conversation with Frank D. Selke, who knew both men well

THERE IS NO REAL EQUIVALENT TO FOSTER HEWITT IN A normal soap opera: a Mr. Clean who keeps on making the best deals.

The drama that engulfed Maple Leaf Gardens in the late 1960s and early 1970s certainly was well-stocked with characters more colorful than Foster. Stafford Smythe and Harold Ballard were tagged in the end as the principal bad guys. Gardens chairman John Bassett had to accept the responsibility of making the unpleasant moves necessary to deal with his former partners. In the end, the job completed, Bassett took Foster along with him, at Foster's request, right out of the Gardens.

The tragedy (for some) and disaster (for others) started in the late summer of 1968 with an anonymous tip to police that some high-level financial hanky-panky was going on at the Gardens. The first public knowledge came in

162

October with an RCMP swoop on the Gardens to pick up
financial records going back for years. Foster was among
the shareholders who were badly shocked by the raid.
Soon he was on the phone to John Bassett, asking, "Do you
know what the hell this is all about?"

Bassett was in the process of finding out. Over the
next two years, as the bad news at the Gardens unfolded,
they were brought closer together than ever, two strong
men of almost laughable contrasts linking up for a common purpose. Both respected the Gardens as a Canadian
institution; both were honest; both were tough—but there
the resemblance ended. Bassett, well over six feet, tow-
ered over Foster. But an even more striking contrast was
in style. Bassett was a dominating figure in any gathering,
not only because of his height but for his flamboyant
hail-fellow-well-met manner. Foster, even with high visi-
bility, rarely dominated anything but hockey broadcasting,
and did not make friends on the spur of the moment.

Actually, Foster thought Bassett was brilliant ("So he
should," Bassett once remarked. "I made him twenty-five
million bucks.") even while his conservative nature, his
closeness with a buck, rebelled. "He thought that I was
extravagant," said Bassett. "I mean, I bought a theater in
Miami, and put money into New York plays—looking for
programs, you know—and always had a permanent charter on a Lear jet . . . all those things he would never do."

Through his friendship with Bassett, Foster knew
more than anyone else except a few Gardens directors
about what kind of case the police were working on in the
winter of 1968–69. The first rumors were that the tax
department was after Smythe, the Gardens president, and
Ballard, executive vice-president, for income-tax evasion.
Soon the unofficial word was that income-tax evasion might
be the least of the charges. By early summer, 1969, even
though no charges had been laid, the Gardens' board of
directors knew at least the broad outline of what had been
going on—and they hated it.

"Most of them wanted to resign," John Bassett said in
a 1985 interview. "I told them they couldn't. In my opinion, it was the best board of directors in the country.

Compare it with CPR or anybody—prominent businessmen were dying to get on that Maple Leaf Gardens board. Now they were dying to get off it, because of what we had found out. I told them that nobody should resign, nobody should sell shares, until we, the company, had recovered the amount of money involved. It was about $400,000, I think."

Instead of the directors resigning, they did what most of them considered to be the next best thing. They asked Smythe and Ballard to resign. Upon refusing, the two were fired. The vote was a tie, the deciding vote cast by Bassett.

Two weeks later, Smythe and Ballard were charged with income-tax evasion. It was another two years, however, before the other shoe fell with an even more resounding crash—charges against Smythe and Ballard of theft and fraud involving cash and securities totaling almost exactly the "about $400,000" that Bassett had specified had to be paid back. Ballard and Smythe were arrested, released on $50,000 bail each and told the case would come to court in October. If convicted, which to those in the know seemed a foregone conclusion, the chieftains would face mandatory jail sentences of not less than two months, with as much as five years a possibility.

Meanwhile, Smythe and Ballard had been working at restitution of the $400,000. Bassett recalls:

> After the money was repaid, the original reason for people like Foster and me to stick around was gone. I talked to Foster. We'd talked frequently over that couple of years, so we'd know what was going on. I told him that I was going to try to get Smythe and Ballard to sell their shares to me at market price. If they did not, then they would have to buy me out.
>
> Foster said, "If they won't sell to you and you sell, will you put my shares in, too, and sell them at the same time?"
>
> I said I would. So Smythe and Ballard and

164

I had our meeting, and I took along Charlie Dubin [now of the Supreme Court of Canada], who was my lawyer at that time. They were not willing to sell to me—and they weren't keen to buy me and Foster out, because they didn't have the money. I made it clear to them that if they didn't buy me out I would launch a civil suit. Dubin explained that possibility to them clearly enough that they borrowed the money to buy me out and to buy out Foster.

In Foster's financial records, this entire incident, his conferences along the way with Bassett and their decision to get out together at the end show only in one brief note about sale of his 12,100 Gardens shares at $30: "effective 31 August 1971."

For Foster, this meant turning his back on forty years of his life. But it was a corner that, in the circumstances, he was ready to turn. The money from his Gardens shares was rolled over immediately to Baton Broadcasting shares, which he was to hold for life. Ballard could find a couple of ways to hurt him yet, but Foster didn't know that.

The denouement of the Smythe-Ballard affair had both tragedy and comedy. Stafford, heartbroken and penitent for the shame he'd brought on his family, died less than two weeks before the October trial date, less than six weeks after the purchase of the Bassett-Hewitt shares. Ballard was sentenced to three years in the penitentiary. He was soon enjoying the fury he caused across the country when, for instance, he compared one of his temporary homes to a good motel, with steaks when desired. The public fell for it like a ton of bricks, manipulated again.

With his son Bill in charge, Ballard continued to be consulted, or even to rule, on major decisions at the Gardens. Messages were relayed up and down the highways to Toronto from the various lockups where Ballard did his time.

It was also typical of him that he didn't start to serve his term until after he had won a fight, early in 1972, for control of the Gardens against a Smythe family group led by Stafford's brother Hugh—and until after he had held lively, Ballard-style court in Moscow in the autumn during the final four games of the first summit series between the Soviets and the NHL.

Although Foster hadn't any stock left to wield in the control battle, it used to amuse him in a rueful way that one reason Doctor Hugh Smythe had not continued the fight was that Conn Smythe was opposed. When some of the old Conn Smythe loyalists went to him and said, "We'll put in the money for Hughie if you say it's all right," Conn said it wasn't all right, that if Hughie won it would take a talented medical man out of circulation and nobody knew whether he'd be a good hockey man.

"He couldn't have done any worse than Ballard," Foster would say with a laugh.

The way the Leafs went down after Punch Imlach was fired by Stafford Smythe in 1969 bothered Foster. It was part of his early disenchantment with the game.

Foster's disenchantment really had begun with the National Hockey League's 1967 expansion from six teams to twelve. He saw that as pure greed. The original teams got $2 million each from the new franchise-holders, with no one caring what would happen to the quality of the game. It was even worse in the second expansion, to 14 teams in 1970, with the new clubs—Vancouver and Buffalo—paying $6 million each and the other twelve splitting the pot. Foster was in favor of making money, all right, but not from the ruining of the game he loved. He felt the skill level had taken a profound dive with the injection of more than a hundred players who couldn't have held a job in the old league. So in the wake of W.A.'s death and Kay's, when he might have been able to lose himself in hockey, he was finding it hardly worth watching.

Living alone in the Rosemary Road home that held so many reminders of Kay and their more than 40 years of marriage contributed to his depression. Most of those who knew him well saw little of that. Bill felt it: "He just wasn't the same even with me. After Mother died, it was

166

just as if he was going through the motions but didn't care much for a lot of things any more."

To help put in the days and nights, Foster spent more time than usual with Bill, Ann, Wendy and their families. Audrey and her husband, Bert Massey, often asked him to dinner. Massey used to say how much he loved having Foster over, because he had such a sense of humor. But Foster confided to all of them that he disliked the end of each evening, with its return to the memories of Rosemary Road.

Then came a change. Foster and Ted Hough had been working friends for many years. When Kay became ill, her cancer not yet diagnosed, Angela Hough, Ted's first wife, was found to have cancer. Her surgery was a severe blow to both of them so as was her lengthy hospitalization. With one then a widower and one soon to be, there were times when the two simply hung together on the road in the grips of their related family tragedies.

With Foster's own family grown, he became something of an honorary godfather to the three Hough children, Mabel, Jim and Sylvia. Foster also maintained his friendship with Angela, which had begun in happier times. He was with Ted's family as a comforting presence when Angela died in 1971. The role of understanding friend to the Hough family never changed in subsequent years, and it is commonly accepted that Ted Hough was one of the closest friends Foster had in his life.

Hough referred laughingly to Foster and himself as the odd couple. They had certain rituals. One came after every hockey game at the Gardens: they'd drive to Fran's Restaurant, a busy twenty-four-hour eatery on St. Clair Avenue near Yonge Street a few miles from the Gardens, in heavy game-night traffic and have hamburgers and coffee or tea. They could have gone to the Gardens Hot Stove Lounge, where Foster would have been glad-handed, but he seemed to get enough of that without having to court it.

Hough: "In other cities, too, we went everywhere together, commiserated each with the other, sometimes drank too much, ate too much." One time in Los Angeles they rented a car and went to Disneyland, then when sundown came and Disneyland closed they spent two hours hunting for their car in the acres of parking lots.

After about two years of Hough and Hewitt being practically inseparable when their schedules permitted, Hough took his two daughters with him to Florida. Foster joined them in a little hotel called the Jolly Roger, full of college kids on their Easter break. It was on that vacation that Foster, laughing, told Ted that they were going to have to get a divorce—he'd met someone, fallen in love and was going to be married.

What had happened was that Foster sometime not long before had taken his two daughters and their husbands to dinner at the Granite Club. Another group in the dining room included people who knew Foster or his daughters. After dinner, some of the diners went home and the survivors joined forces. It was then that Foster met Joan Lang, a lively and attractive woman in her early forties. Foster asked Joan to dance. They danced well together. When the time came to leave, Joan asked several of the group, including Foster, to come back to her place for a nightcap.

Joan, more than twenty-five years younger than Foster, was divorced, and at that time all four of her children still lived with her in her big North Toronto home surrounded by gardens. She certainly knew who Foster Hewitt was. One of her sons had got a high mark in an English class for an imitation he had done of Foster at work. But hockey, CKFH or Foster's other interests, including vice-presidencies at CFTO-TV and associated companies, were not discussed that evening. In fact, Joan thought, he hasn't said a darn thing about himself at all.

They were in her kitchen fixing drinks when she looked at Foster, deadpan, and said, "What exactly do you do for a living?"

Foster probably hadn't been asked that question for nearly fifty years. He looked at her to see if she was kidding and then decided she was not.

"Well, I broadcast a few hockey games from time to time," he said mildly.

Joan had her own home, many friends and a lively

168

family. She played golf in summer at the Rosedale Golf Club and curled in winter at the Granite Club with, she says, no intention of marrying again. She didn't really change her mind even after she and Foster began going out a lot together. "But he wanted to be married and he really was wonderful to be with, so after a while I said yes."

On Monday, 29 May 1972, about a year after they met, they were married in Christ Church Anglican in Etobicoke, with front-page pictures in many newspapers. The one in the Montreal *Gazette* under a photograph of the glowing couple read:

> Foster Hewitt, Canada's "voice of hockey" since the twenties, was married yesterday to Joan Darlie Lang in Toronto. It was the second marriage for both. The new Mrs. Hewitt, a divorcee, has four children, two boys and two girls. Hewitt, 68 [he was really sixty-nine] was a widower with three children: Mrs. Frank M. Somerville, Mrs. Barry Rowan and Foster William Alfred, known as Bill, who broadcasts hockey on television; Hewitt still broadcasts the games on radio. Since his first broadcast on 23 March 1923, Hewitt has broadcast thousands of games, making his name synonymous with hockey throughout Canada.

At the time, Joan's oldest son, Stu, was nineteen. He later became a football star at Queen's and in Edmonton. Her other children were Sherry, seventeen; Donald, fifteen; and Barbara, thirteen.

How did Foster and Joan decide whose house to live in? Not especially quietly.

"He wanted to live in his and I wanted to live in mine," Joan explained. "But I had the four children, and although Stu was about to go to Queen's and Sherry to school in Switzerland, that left two lively kids, and his house was full of antiques."

169

But there was more to the decision than that. The Rosemary Road house had been in Kay's name, with the provision that Foster could live in it for life. Then it would revert to Kay's estate, meaning that if anything happened to Foster, Joan would have no place to live.

Foster could see that as well as Joan could. He moved into Joan's home, taking some of his favorite furniture along and was to live there for the rest of his life. But at the time of the marriage, when Bill mentioned to Foster that it might be a good idea to sell the Rosemary Road house and wind up Kay's estate, Foster demurred. "It's not a thing to decide too quickly," he said. "A person shouldn't abandon his roots, or his lines of, if necessary."

So the home was rented to staff from the British consulate until the early 1980s, always there to move into if Foster ever decided he needed a place to go.

In the next few years Bill drove by the Rosemary Road house from time to time. There was sometimes a pang of memory. He naturally wasn't as much in his father's company socially any more; perhaps a few times a year at Joan's home for dinner, the conversation general, nothing like when Kathleen was alive and the family home was there to drop in to at any time. "No matter how hard you try, nobody replaces your mother, and as close to my mother as I was, I couldn't be objective. He just said to me one day, 'I'm going to get married.' I said, 'Fine, Dad. Good luck.' As far as Joan was concerned, really, we were at long range."

17

THE MARCH
ON MOSCOW

● ● ●

"Foster really tore a strip off me in that 1972
series between the Russians and the NHL. I'd
always thought until then that he was a mild
little guy. But we're in Moscow at the Intourist
Hotel and of course I knew Foster and we're
all in the lobby, everybody else getting ready
to go to the rink, when I mentioned, happy and
excited, really, that I had traded my hockey
tickets for two at the Bolshoi ballet.

"He was furious. I've never seen him that
way. Blasted me in front of everybody. 'Millions of people back home in Canada would
give their right arms to be going to this hockey
game! And you trade your tickets for a bloody
Russian ballet! You oughta be ashamed of
yourself!' Then he turned and stomped away.
I never got over that. I don't think he did,
either."

—A ballet fan, Toronto

AT THE TIME FOSTER AND JOAN LANG MARRIED, THE FIRST
hockey-summit series was being planned. Team Canada,
really a team of NHL all-stars who were, what's more,
Canadians, was to play the national team of the Soviet

Union four games in Canada early in September and another four in Moscow near the end of the month.

It would be the biggest event ever in the hockey world. There was a lot of back rooming and infighting about commercial aspects of the rich television rights, but none about who would be behind the microphone. Johnny Esaw, the CTV network vice-president (sports), eventually wound up as executive producer of the series for television. When someone asked him if having a man nearly seventy years old handling the play-by-play was really a good idea, Esaw replied, "Who else is there, for a series like this?"

Ted Hough, as head of the Canadian Sports Network, agreed. Foster was still doing radio but less and less television, and from time to time mentioned full retirement. Hough's idea was that for the greatest broadcaster, the greatest series would be a suitable last hurrah. Foster was happy. He had been wanting this series, the best against the best, for nearly twenty years.

Nothing to match the excitement of this series had ever happened in Canada; rarely anywhere, in any sport. The last time Canada had beaten the Soviets at hockey was in the world championships of 1961, with the Trail Smoke Eaters as the Canadian representatives. Nine years of regular beatings later, Canada said to hell with it and withdrew from world competition. The ultimate Canadian policy, then and now, is for world championships to be decided by the best against the best; the best, in Canada's terms, meaning professionals.

It took two years before the Soviets, finally convinced that it was the only way to get Canada back on the ice, gave in.

The agreement for the series was made between the Soviet hockey committee and Hockey Canada. R. Alan Eagleson was the key Canadian and called the shots. As director of the NHL Players' Association, he had convinced the players that this series was worth doing, and that it would contribute a considerable profit to their pension plan. As a member of Hockey Canada's international committee, he could look out for the welfare of his gladiators from that side, too. If he'd only been president of MacLaren

172

Advertising or even the Canadian Sports Network at the same time, there wouldn't have been any hitch.

As it was, there was one major item not in his control for a little while—the sale of television rights. Ted Hough, on behalf of the Canadian Sports Network, with Foster aboard and a respectable lineup of sponsors waiting in the wings, offered Hockey Canada $500,000 plus everything above a certain level (not disclosed) of commercial income, which couldn't be given as more than a speculative figure at that time. According to Eagleson, the deal was about to be accepted by Hockey Canada, without his knowledge, until he had a tip from someone at the CBC.

Eagleson in action in such a crisis is a sight to see (not bad for sound effects, either). He figured that a half-million plus the possibility of pie in the sky wasn't enough and that the rights-buyer could pay a good deal more and still make a profit. He accordingly got on the phone and put together a deal, combining some of Harold Ballard's money and some of Bobby Orr's, to bid for the rights. The bid was $750,000. The Canadian Sports Network bowed out, but their plan to use Foster happily survived into a new deal that had the CTV network (under Eagleson's general chairmanship, of course) in command of an attraction about to draw the biggest television audiences in Canadian history.

In subsequent years, those watching the almost-routine arranging of hockey games or series involving the world's two major hockey powers tend to forget the drama that surrounded that first summit-series. One element in the makeup of the Canadian team was the subject of intervention by then prime minister Pierre Trudeau, who called a meeting at which he asked a delegation from Hockey Canada to include Bobby Hull on the team.

Hull was the greatest player of the time but had just left the Chicago Black Hawks to sign with the Winnipeg Jets of the new World Hockey Association.

Being out of the NHL, he at first was said not to be eligible. This did not stick for long. Hull soon was invited privately by Eagleson and accepted, but the news got out before it could be made official. Eagleson said later he could have handled the matter and included Hull if others, including Hull and the prime minister, had given him time to grease the skids or oil the troubled waters, or do whatever needed doing.

Instead, it became a combined public outrage (there were bumper stickers reading "To Russia With Hull") and political issue (We hear you, voters). The prime minister sent telegrams to NHL president Clarence Campbell and Players Association president Red Berenson urging Hull's inclusion. By the time the furor died down, the NHL's nose was so far out of joint that there could be no backing down and no possibility of Hull's inclusion, prime ministers and public clamor notwithstanding.

For Foster, the series was like having a Stanley Cup playoff in September. Apart from the occasional business meeting, Foster and Joan spent a restful honeymoon summer, much of it in Beaverton. In August, Team Canada went into training in Maple Leaf Gardens, while they lived at the Westbury Hotel. Many players looked forward to the series as something of a lark. They'd been told, and had told themselves for years, that when the Russians skated out against *real* Canadian hockey players they'd never know what hit them. Some sportswriters predicted an eight-game sweep, and not by the Soviets. Well.

It was interesting that even when the NHL took an early two-goal lead in the first game in Montreal, Foster didn't count out the Soviets—who eventually won 7–3 with the NHL all-stars hanging on the ropes. They were in a state of shock, as was the television audience that had watched the debacle.

The series moved across the country to a rising clamor: a 4–1 win for Canada in Toronto; a 4–4 tie in Winnipeg; 5–3 for the Soviets in Vancouver. Foster, rarely seen in most of those cities except on television screens, signed hundreds of autographs and in his understated way began to sound like the conscience of Canadian hockey asking, what the hell's going on?

After the Vancouver game on 8 September, the teams took a two-week break before the final four games of the series in Moscow. By then, general opinion was that the

Canadians, having done so badly in their own country, would lose quickly in Moscow.

There were some humorous aspects to the gloom about Moscow. There wouldn't only be the strangeness of the foreign strand to contend with, the nation was told gravely. An advance party had discovered no Coca-Cola in Moscow! T-bone steaks were unknown, at least by that name. And the toilet paper! In Canada, softer stuff than that was used to prepare floors for fresh coats of varnish. Canadians were informed that their own versions of all these essential items would be shipped to Moscow to be on hand when required.

It should be stressed, however, that Team Canada had become deadly serious. Those players, the absolute cream of our crop, knew better than anyone what they were up against.

For the most part, the great Canadian march on Moscow in late September 1972 was unusually democratic. Some broadcast technicians flew in early, and Eagleson had gone with the team to Sweden where they regrouped, played a couple of exhibitions and coped with jet lag in stages instead of all at once. A stream of lively air charters carried everyone else, including Foster and Joan Hewitt, across the Atlantic. The open bar, the parading up and down aisles to stop and talk to friends or introduce oneself to celebrities—it was like a throwback to a once-common Canadian custom that few aboard had ever experienced: the old railway specials to see playoff hockey or football. But this time the special carried the fans through eight time zones.

When they landed in Moscow in time for resumption of hockey hostilities and were deployed to various Moscow hotels, Foster and Joan drew one of the better ones, the Intourist near Red Square. But their room was not what either of them was used to. "Crappy," Joan called it. "There was a broken window above Foster's bed. I was always waiting for a storm that would drench us both."

In Moscow, Joan saw Foster for the first time as the complete professional, with hockey taking precedence over everything. The games were two days apart, and even days off were full of arguments over referees, practice time and other excursions that Foster had to keep track of to do his job.

Every game day he went early to the Luzhniki Sports Palace to get ready for his broadcast. Joan would look at the sights with other hockey tourists and board a bus in late afternoon for the rink. Beer, other drinks and food were available at long counters at the rink, and the uproar in the Canada section, the cheers and blowing of noise-makers and flag-waving, was answered more or less good-naturedly by the Russian fans.

For Foster, the first Moscow game was two periods of high excitement that ended with Canada ahead 3–0. In the third period, his voice had to rise above the crowd noise as the Soviets made it 3–1. Canada increased the lead to 4–1, and then in five and a half desperate minutes, the Soviets ran in four goals, to lead 5–4. The game ended at that, meaning that the Soviets, who had now won three games and tied one out of the first five, needed only one more win to take the series.

The broadcast-crew meetings in the next few days were subdued, then began to reflect a glimmer of hope, then more than a glimmer—but the rest is hockey history. Canada won the sixth game 3–2, with Paul Henderson, a Toronto Maple Leaf in normal times, scoring the winning goal. They won the seventh game 4–3 with Henderson again scoring the winning goal that tied the series.

The eighth game is remembered by many who were listening in Canada as Foster's finest. The goals went back and forth but the Soviets led 5–3 at the end of the second period.

Just before 2:27 of the third period, Foster reported:

Pete Mahovlich is going down left wing, keeps on going into the corner, is bumped back of the net, centered in front, here's Esposito getting it. . . . *They score! Esposito!* [Crowd roars] Esposito scores for Canada, from Peter Mahovlich! [Crowd still roaring] If you don't succeed the first time, try, try again!

176

Ten minutes and twenty-some seconds later, just before 12:56, Canada still trailing 5–4, Foster called:

Mishakov at center knocked the puck back of the Canadian goal. Park is trying to come out on the left side. . . . A long pass to Phil Esposito! Going in! *He shoots!* Oh, right in front of the net! Esposito banged at it! Here's another shot by Cournoyer. . . . *He scores!* [Shouting above the crowd] Canada has tied it up! Esposito makes an incredible individual effort on this goal! I can't say enough, look at him fight for the puck [this was on the television replay] and get it back in front of the net after having missed it once himself! And I believe it's Yvan Cournoyer who gets the goal.

Finally, leading up to the last goal, starting in the second-last minute:

The Canadian team went into a huddle there, which seems to be a little unusual. [word lost] they're really fighting. The puck comes up at center ice. Vasiliev carries it back into his zone, to Shadrin who missed it. Peter Mahovlich is at center, driving it into the Soviet zone. Liapkin gets there first. Cournoyer just touched it. Savard, getting it at center ice, clearing it off a skate. It goes into the Canadian zone. Yakushev, a dangerous player, is belted on that play. Cournoyer rolled it out, Vasiliev going back to get it. There's 1:02 left in the game.

A cleared pass on the far side. Liapkin rolled one to Savard. Savard clears a pass to Stapleton. He cleared to the open wing to Cournoyer. *Here's a shot!* Henderson made a wild stab for it and fell. *Here's another shot, right in front— They score! Henderson scores for Canada!* And the fans and the team are going wild! *Henderson,* right in front of the Soviet goal with thirty-four seconds left in the game!

That was hockey when we were learning how good the Russians were, and they were learning how good we were. It was also Foster, calling that goal by Paul Henderson as it would be heard a thousand times or more on radio and television specials to come, a broadcast to remember him by.

18

FOSTER BEATS CANCER BUT SAYS SOME GOOD-BYES

●●●

"As soon as Dad came back from Moscow we got together and he said to me, 'After that, what do you do for an encore? Nothing! Absolutely nothing can compare to that. Or if it does, let somebody else do it.' "
—Bill Hewitt, in conversation in 1985

BILL TOOK THAT AS FOSTER'S FIRST UNEQUIVOCAL INDICAtion that sometime, perhaps not far down the road, he would stop broadcasting NHL games. But there was still some ego left, some things to be proved. In a few months after the return from Moscow, Foster celebrated the fiftieth anniversary of his first hockey broadcast from that airless glass booth at the Mutual Street Arena.

There were other reasons to stay on. Joan had been in her early forties when they married, and Foster sixtynine. Some men at that age are over the hill, but not Foster. He was the living example of the good that comes from a career of following one's heart's desire. Foster had always looked and acted younger than he was, and he now had the opportunity to show his new wife how the master of his craft went about his business. Besides, Joan traveled with him sometimes. In the bars and restaurants he had so thoroughly scouted around the league they could

179

have fun. If he was ever to have a last hurrah, this was
it.

So Foster and Bob Gordon kept on making their quick
trips out for single road games. On longer road trips, Joan
often went along. Then something happened that made
Foster consider retirement, at least from hockey broadcasting.

By 1974 he was having increasing trouble with his
prostate gland, a condition not uncommon in men much
younger than his nearly seventy-two years. An examination
brought bad news: he had cancer of the prostate. There
were two courses he could have followed. One would be
an operation, an attempt to remove the cancer. The second
would be radium treatments. He chose the radium treatments, painful and debilitating sessions designed to eliminate the disease. They naturally caused a massive disloca-
tion of his normal active life, but when the treatments
ended they seemed to have worked. Still, it was then that
he discussed retirement seriously with the Canadian Sports
Network.

Ted Hough discouraged anything that would bring
about a publicized retirement and seem to put paid to
Foster's career. Foster eventually agreed to a gentle kind
of phasing down, a reduction of his work load while he
remained available for special assignments. He would broadcast some games, but Ron Hewat, by then a senior executive at CKFH, would handle most of the radio play-by-play
and Bill would continue to do the television.

It was about then that another person, eventually to
become a close friend, entered Foster's life. Fred Dixon, a
cheerful and affable man, had been vice-president of finance and administration for his family's company, whose
business was the manufacture and distribution of paint-
brushes and a number of other items used in the paint
business. The company auditor, Donald Hill, was also
auditor for CKFH. When his family sold its business, Dixon,
then in his late forties, looked for something else to do.
Foster was looking around for someone to run the finances
at CKFH. Donald Hill got them together, they liked one
another and Fred Dixon was appointed comptroller of

CKFH. The station's offices by then had moved out of the studio to another building only a block or so away on Yonge Street, coincidentally on the eleventh floor of a building also occupied by MacLaren Advertising and the Canadian Sports Network.

So for the last ten years of Foster's life, he and Fred Dixon spent almost every working day together, with so much happening that a biographer may be forgiven for wishing that someone had been taking notes or keeping a daily diary. No one was. Basically, except for secretaries and a few others, Foster Hewitt and Fred Dixon, with Bill's input as well, were the operating heads of the house that Foster had built. Neither was wedded to a no-change policy. In fact, in the next deal Foster made, he decided to stop, this once anyway, being a loner.

With the Toronto Blue Jays due to enter the American Baseball League in 1977, Foster was approached at CKFH in 1976 to carry the Blue Jay games and set up an Ontario network to take the word to outside communities. This practice is common among baseball teams and is always a money-maker, pleasing to advertisers and fans alike.

Foster knew CKFH could handle the job of flagship station for the Blue Jay network but felt he would need an additional sales organization as well. It was auditor Donald Hill who suggested that a joint venture would be the best financial arrangement. A company called Opex, which was in effect the sales division of the Montreal-based company called Telemedia, owned radio stations in Quebec and so had the know-how. Soon, Hewpex, a combination of Hewittdale, Foster's holding company, and Opex was born. Telemedia later added another company, Telmed, on its side. Basically Opex did the selling and CKFH did the broadcasting. It was an immediate success, CKFH covering the Toronto area and a string of smaller stations ensuring that almost everybody interested in Blue Jay baseball could listen to pregame shows, postgame shows and play-by-play. It was another profitable area for CKFH, just at a time when Foster was about to lose his role in what had been a fifty-year tradition.

Generations of hockey fans had grown up hearing Foster Hewitt and the Toronto Maple Leafs several times a week on CKFH. The tradition ended in divorce. A mere matter of money severed Foster's long-standing connection with the Toronto Maple Leafs. The newspapers were full of letters lamenting the change and lambasting Harold Ballard of the Gardens for being a money-grubbing so-and-so with no care for what he was doing to hockey fans.

The people who might have prevented it were long gone from the Gardens. Conn Smythe, the other side of that old handshake agreement on hockey broadcasting, had resigned from the Gardens board of directors years earlier in protest when Ballard booked a fight involving Muhammad Ali; to old soldier Smythe, the fact that Ali was the best heavyweight in the world was not as important as the fact that he had refused to serve in the United States Army. So Smythe's voice wasn't there to stand up for the old association.

Stafford, a true Smythe in many important ways, might have counted the Foster Hewitt–Gardens tradition as meaning more than a few dollars. But he was dead.

So only Ballard was left, his penitentiary term behind him, when the agreement on radio rights came up for renewal in 1978. As the chief shareholder of Maple Leaf Gardens, Limited, and already with the one rap against him for doing shareholders out of their full share, his could have been simply a business decision. The radio rights were worth money: who offered the most? But in other matters Ballard had been known to let sentiment control his actions, so one can only assume that he didn't have any sentiment to spare for Foster Hewitt.

Was that year's auction of radio rights suddenly, for once, pure business, or at least partly a reflection of Ballard's feeling that Foster had turned his back when Ballard was in trouble with the law? Perhaps it was a little bit of both.

Foster often told Fred Dixon that he and Ballard had been friends for a long time before the friendship ended, and that he wished he could get back to the relationship they once had. But, as Dixon said, "There was a friction there. They wouldn't even cross the street to say hello. Whenever Foster was sick, Harold called him, yet they never seemed to get together. All I do know is that certain types of trouble people got into, Foster didn't accept."

Foster, as the Gardens director of broadcasting, had controlled the radio rights from the beginning. Then when CKFH was started, he had made a deal for the station to get full control. He first paid $5,000 for radio rights, then $10,000 and as time went on up to $25,000. Once a few years earlier another group had outbid him but had failed to come up with the money before the season started, so Foster had moved back in.

By the time of the latest renewal, Foster's offer was in the range of $40,000 to $45,000 for one year. But the CKO radio all-news network was being set up, based in Toronto. Needing something to establish itself quickly in the Toronto market, probably even aware that Foster had used the same technique when getting CKFH started twenty-five years earlier, the CKO people bid $125,000. Foster matched that. Then CKO offered $250,000 for two years and agreed to a little Ballard extra: they would also buy two of the plush new Gardens hospitality boxes then being built, where corporations could entertain customers from nice little bars and comfortable chairs well above the madding crowd. Foster's judgment was that a guy might try paying $125,000 for one year and see how he made out, but a two-year commitment at that price was too much. He checked out of the bidding.

Bill was running CKFH at that time but Foster's voice was still the one everyone jumped to. Station CKO got the rights. Public protests were loud and long. The outraged traditionalists had their grumpy say: CKO was only on FM, so people with ordinary AM home sets no longer could get the Leafs games.

Foster was in excellent health at the time, seemingly fully recovered from his radium treatments and the cancer. But his working days no longer included any but occasional broadcasting appearances. He and Bill even casually talked over the option of selling CKFH and perhaps both retiring at the same time. Foster and Joan were spending happy summers in Beaverton, and while he sometimes chafed at relative inactivity after so many years of never having enough hours in the day, he seemed content.

In 1978 he was back before the microphones at the game marking the anniversary of Hockey Night in Canada. It was the show's twenty-fifth year on television. That was his last NHL hockey broadcast ever.

He was increasingly concerned about the way CKFH was going. He was chairman then, with Bill vice-chairman and Ron Hewat president. Foster's uneasiness about CKFH was based partly on the relationship between his son and Ron Hewat. Hewat's hard work and ambition had taken him to the top operating job in the station, sometimes—it seemed to onlookers—to the detriment of Bill. It was no easy task for a non-Hewitt, even named Hewat (and pronounced Hew-att to emphasize the slight difference in the names) to make his way to the top of CKFH. But Bill's own nature, easy-going and generous, had helped make possible this change. Although Foster left no correspondence or other written material to support this belief, people close to him thought that he simply wasn't happy about the way CKFH was being run.

Fred Dixon still saw Foster every day. Foster came to the office around eleven, and usually did not leave until six. Most of his day would be spent checking the progress and profit of his investments. But it was customary that late in the day he and Fred Dixon would confer. One evening Foster brought up the matter of selling CKFH.

Dixon recalls: "He told me he had thought about it, and had been contacted several times by people who wanted to buy. It was then he told me that if certain things at CKFH didn't go the way he wanted them to, he would sell—and that things were approaching that point. He said, 'I really don't want to give up but. . . .'

"One night just before Christmas, I think it was a year or two later, Foster was getting ready to go with Joan to Florida. He called me into his office and said, 'I want you to do me a favor while I'm in Florida. I want you to entertain the idea of selling the station. Call in Donald

Hill. The two of you see what you can come up with and we'll talk when I get back.' "

Foster had left a couple of names of people to be contacted. One was Philippe de Gaspé Beaubien of Telemedia, the company he'd been associated with in the Blue Jay network. Dixon got in touch with de Gaspé Beaubien. He showed a keen interest and quickly became the prime prospect.

When Foster and Joan came home from Florida, Foster also met with de Gaspé Beaubien. Talks progressed and they came very close to an agreement.

Dixon: "In fact, we were to have one more meeting that might tie it all up, in Donald Hill's office. The Telemedia people were there, headed by de Gaspé Beaubien, as well as Foster, Donald Hill and myself. The plan at the time was for Foster to stay in CKFH as a partner. Then the talks took a twist that Foster definitely didn't like—they were questioning our claims about the station's signal. Their contention was that we weren't able to deliver the audience coverages to the east and west that we contended we could. Foster had his own idea of what the station could do and how he wanted to make the deal and said if things weren't going to happen that way, the deal was off. Bang. And it was. So they walked away from it and we walked away from it."

Then another prospect entered the picture. Before dealing with the new prospect, Foster brought in an engineer from Quebec to check the signal's coverages. The engineer found that the signal did have some problems by one method of measurement, but was very good by another, contrary to Telemedia's contention.

By some means, Philippe de Gaspé Beaubien found out about the engineer's report and that another contender might be close to making a deal. At that point, in June 1980, he hurried to Toronto, walked into Foster's office, sat himself down and said, "I'm not leaving this office until we have an agreement."

They talked; Foster called in his lawyers; de Gaspé Beaubien called in his. A letter of intent was drafted then and there. The major change was in the conditions of sale.

In the interval since the first talks, Foster had decided he no longer would remain as a partner. He wanted out of CKFH entirely. So it was a straight buy. The exact price was not announced, but guesses in the four-million-dollar range were considered not out of line.

There were still loose ends to tidy up, an application to the Canadian Radio and Telecommunications Commission to transfer the license, hearings in Toronto in October, final approval in February to go ahead with the sale and the change of call letters to CJCL.

19

ON THE ROAD AGAIN

●●●

"Every place the train stopped there would be
these huge crowds, and do you think they
wanted to see me, or Horner, or Jackson, or
Clancy? No, they'd want to see that scrawny
little bastard, Hewitt. We'd all parade out and,
'Where's Foster?' they'd say."
  —Charlie Conacher, in the 1930s

A BIOGRAPHER STRIVING FOR BALANCE (THERE MUST BE
somebody out there who didn't like Hewitt) falls gratefully
on the snarly nature of Conacher's remark, then realizes
it's still an accolade. The worst reaction to Foster on
record is one man's memory that when Foster cried, "He
scores!" his father would mutter, "Fishmouth!" But the
man's father was a Montreal fan. A Regina woman said
bluntly that Foster was never a factor in her household.
But she also mentioned that she had to get married on a
Saturday morning, early, or nobody would have come—the
Saskatchewan Roughriders were playing that afternoon. A
football family, obviously. The overwhelming commonal-
ity was, as Earl McRae wrote years later:

> To those of a certain generation, his name will
> always evoke a kind of mystique: of winter

187

nights and farm lights burning on darkened prairies; of frozen ponds and rivers and the thin cries of children with wind-scoured faces, playing until it was too dark to play, playing until mother's voice called them home for supper. And yes, of nights around the old corner radio with the glowing green eye; of toast and cocoa and snug pajamas and the warm, amber ambience of a lamp. "Hello, Canada! and hockey fans in the United States and Newfoundland. . . ."

I remember Bobby Hull telling me how he'd run home Saturday nights from the Bay of Quinte . . . hang his steaming socks by the kitchen stove and gather with chums and the family to await Foster Hewitt. "The streets were always empty," said Hull. "Everybody was home, tuned in to Hockey Night in Canada. When Foster came on, I literally trembled with excitement. That high-pitched, nasal twang; when I met him years later, it was like meeting God.

Did that feeling last when Foster was no longer part of the weekly magic?

In 1977 the Canadian government changed the name of Canada's birthday holiday from Dominion Day to Canada Day. Opposition to the change had festered for years, seen as it was by Canadians of British blood, even generations back, as part of the gradual and unwelcome severing of Canada's links with Britain. The government, wishing to overcome the opposition and build a new tradition around the new name, set aside funds for Canada Day celebrations across the country. Major cities were encouraged, financially and otherwise, to arrange patriotic festivities for the day. For smaller centers, especially those far from cities, the government's plan was to send out groups of touring celebrities to be interviewed by local newspapers, radio and television, who would talk up Canada Day.

In Ontario's north, the government thought a tour by famous hockey players would make the right impact. Hockey Night in Canada seemed the natural nominee to lay this on. The organizational task fell mainly on Foster's former traveling companion, Bob Gordon, along with commentator Brian McFarlane and Frank D. Selke, Canadian Sports Network vice-president.

Gordon started out with a list of hockey stars to invite. But hockey stars are difficult to pin down in summer, especially on short notice. They have their own family holidays planned, promotional events contracted for, charity baseball games sponsored by breweries or other companies. Money wouldn't move them, either. Gordon tried several Leafs stars: Darryl Sittler, Lanny McDonald and on through the list. He was turned down. "To make a long story short, I couldn't get any hockey players to commit themselves for ten days, even if I offered them the world. Two thousand a day sort of thing. 'Oh, I don't want to go for ten days.' "

He did get Randy Carlyle, a defenseman with the Toronto Maple Leafs. Carlyle is a fair size but by himself would not quite constitute a busload of celebrities.

"So I think, What am I going to do? We've accepted, I've got to do something. Then I thought, Why not Foster Hewitt? How many hockey players are as well known as Foster Hewitt and King Clancy?"

He called both and outlined the plan. Ted Hough reinforced the invitation to Foster. The probable clincher was that wives were invited. In the end the celebrity party, to be shepherded by Gordon along a campaign trail laid out by a Canadian government press agent, Mary K. Patrick, included Foster and Joan Hewitt, King Clancy and his wife Rae, Frank Selke and his wife Red and Randy Carlyle. In addition to the high hockey profiles of Foster, Clancy and Carlyle, Frank Selke bore one of the most famous hockey names of all and had been familiar to television audiences as a long-time intermission host in Montreal Canadiens' telecasts.

No expense was spared. The fact that someone else was paying the shot didn't do any harm to Foster's and

Clancy's peace of mind, either. A full-sized Voyageur bus was converted to something like a big motor home. A banner stretched along each side for almost the full length of the bus reading: "Canada, I Want To Shake Your Hand." A Canadian flag was lashed across the front. (In northern Ontario the lines were cut and the flag stolen, no doubt to fly somewhere on Canada Day.) Reverse seats had been arranged comfortably around a couple of tables, and a dressing-room area was curtained off at the back. Two refrigerator-type coolers were aboard, loaded with liquor, beer, soft drinks and ice.

The grand takeoff took place from a shopping plaza on the north edge of Toronto, covered by CFTO but by no other television station, the publicly owned CBC having decided not to start celebrating Canada Day just yet.

As the bus headed north in the late-afternoon traffic, the first clink of ice was heard, drinks were poured and the party settled down to ten days of helping the government get its point across. A few hours later, Foster and Clancy were being interviewed by North Bay television in the lobby of the Empire Hotel against a backdrop of flags and surrounded by citizens thrusting out their autograph books.

The next day established the tour's modus operandi: newspaper photographers, a meeting with Mayor Merle Dickerson of North Bay (in a Hawaiian beach-boy sports shirt), signing the guest book, signing autographs, some main-streeting by Foster, King and Carlyle with Joan Hewitt and Rae Clancy following the crowds. By the time the bus headed out for New Liskeard other patterns had been set: a few drinks, a lot of looking at scenery, a lot of sandwiches and fried chicken, occasional glimpses of moose and, once, a timber wolf.

Everybody soon had seats staked out. Foster was cordial and jovial with all comers, but rarely moved from his place beside Joan. But each time the bus stopped he would be first out, chatting about hockey with old-timers, laughing his cheerful laugh at memories they evoked, stepping on stage again as he must have done forty years earlier with Charlie Conacher and the old Leafs. For those who found themselves next to Foster in his casual sports jacket and Clancy in his Maple Leaf blue, it was like old home week on the Hot Stove League; talking about hockey with people who knew the answers.

After a hard day when the schedule didn't leave much time between arrival and dinner, Foster refused to be hurried. He and Joan would invite a few people to their room. If this ran over the time set aside for dinner, so be it. They would arrive late and happy.

Once when the bus stopped at a sign saying that from there on all rivers flowed north, Foster instructed the others on the physical structures of the Great Divide.

Eventually the northern communities began to run together: New Liskeard, Cobalt, Kirkland Lake, Timmins, Cochrane; legion halls, community centers, curling rinks, city halls, old-timers with old hockey sticks to be signed, pictures of long-gone hockey games, screaming school-children. Gordon noted in his diary: "What ego-building this must be for Clancy and Foster—everybody recognizes them and is delighted to see them."

In Smooth Rock Falls, Foster apparently decided to lay to rest once and for all the legend that he never picked up a check. During the morning proceedings he asked a town official to lay on lunch, which would be on him. Soon the travelers were ushered into a dining hall set with a lavish display of Chinese food.

Gordon's diary: "The food kept coming and the gang kept eating, an unbelievable amount. I stood up and on behalf of the group thanked everybody for their hospital-ity and for the food. I also made a big point of calling out from the kitchen the Chinese family who cooked the lunch, and we all thanked them and got back on the bus and headed for Kapuskasing about an hour behind schedule.

"As I walked through the bus a little later Foster said, 'Bob, let me know how much that meal cost, since I asked the guy to arrange it, and let me pay for it.'

"I said, 'Pay for it? I had no idea we were paying for it.' "

There are probably people in Smooth Rock Falls still

willing to believe anything they hear about Foster Hewitt being close with his money.

In Kapuskasing a dentist who was drunk offered the ultimate in hospitality, reeling up to Foster with, "Hey, Foshter, I love you so much I'd take out all your teeth for nothing."

At Hearst, in pouring rain and with a couple of blocks to go between the motel and the place where dinner had been arranged, Foster and Joan held one of their happy hours in their room, all present. Then the hungriest were ferried to dinner. Time passed. Several of the party, including the Hewitts, didn't show up. When they did, everyone quite cheerful, Foster spilled part of a bottle of steak sauce on his pants. With a calm born of facing everything a hockey trip of old could offer, he promptly picked up a salt shaker and salted his pants liberally from the knees to the hips. "Best thing for cleaning soiled pants," he explained quietly to his fascinated audience.

The rest of the evening was pretty good. A couple of local councilwomen had showed up at dinner and joined in the festivities, which included, unknown to most but not all of the travelers, two naked disco dancers, a man and a woman, in an adjoining nightclub. The councilwomen wanted everyone to visit city hall and sign the guest book. Northern parties sometimes tend to last a while, given compatible company. At city hall the mixed local and traveling crowd took over the council chambers and for two hours had Randy Carlyle in the dock while Foster, Clancy and others debated and renegotiated his contract with the Leafs, cutting his pay.

The next morning a subdued busload headed west to Trans Canada Pipeline Station 86, on a trail off the main highway. The station had a total of eight houses, five occupied, one with a spread of coffee and food that revived everyone. (Foster apparently required revival less than everyone else except Clancy, the total abstainer.)

Longlac, Geraldton, on toward Nipigon. . . . On the Nipigon leg the bus was stopped by a police cruiser. The constable who got on the bus obviously suspected he had been the victim of a practical joke: his dispatcher had told him to stop a bus containing Foster Hewitt and King Clancy and tell them their rooms were confirmed at the Red Oak in Thunder Bay. He didn't believe Foster and Clancy were really there until he saw for himself. He went away with autographs and flags.

That was a Saturday. The Queen's Plate race was on television. Clancy arranged to skip out away from the local reception for a while, to a local tavern to watch the race. He was taken there by a town official only to find a crowd of locals watching a snooker game. The official asked if he could switch the television to the horse race, because this gentleman here was King Clancy of the Toronto Maple Leafs and he would like to see the Queen's Plate.

The answer, delivered by spokesmen for the snooker fans: "We don't give a (bleep) if he's (bleeping) King Kong, but he sure as (bleep) isn't going to turn off the (bleeping) snooker for some (bleeping) horse race." So Clancy didn't see the horse race.

Apart from incidents like that, there was a sameness about many of the stops. But it was all, in a way, a tribute to the old hockey that had nurtured Foster and King Clancy and many others; whatever it did for Canada Day was more or less incidental.

Maybe the stop at Fort Frances was the funniest. The bus had arrived late the night before from Kenora. Everybody was still asleep the next morning when the phone rang in Foster's room. The Toronto CBC station was on the line, wanting to interview him live in a couple of minutes about the tour so far.

"Okay," Foster said, "give me a minute to wake up and then we can start."

On the air a minute later, Foster called the interviewer by his first name and, sounding bright and wide awake, said, "We're having a wonderful trip. I'm speaking to you now from Chapleau. . . ."

In the next room Bob Gordon heard this much through the thin wall at the head of his bed. He was about to yell, "No, Foster! Fort Frances!" when he heard Joan call from her bed, very sleepily, "Psst, Foster dear, we're not in Chapleau, we're in Wawa."

Gordon listened to the rest of the interview, which included a typical Foster Hewitt story. Station CKFH was into its first season of Blue Jay broadcasts and Foster never could resist a chance for a plug. The interviewer asked him if there was a lot of hockey talk going on during the trip. Foster: "Yeah, some, but a lot of people get the Blue Jays, you know, on the Hewpex network, through CKFH—and they like to talk baseball a lot, too."

Thunder Bay, Nipigon, Atikokan, Marathon, Dryden, White River, Wawa, Chapleau, Blind River, Elliot Lake, Espanola, Copper Cliff, Sturgeon Falls. . . . Foster always said it wasn't a bad way for a guy to spend nine days in June when he was coming up to his seventy-fifth birthday. Some of his satisfaction must have been in knowing, however deeply buried the realization was, that Charlie Conacher, long gone, and Bobby Hull, years beyond his "trembling with excitement" around the radio in the home near the Bay of Quinte, were still right.

20

THE BAD SPELL

●●●

"Foster came to me one day, getting close to his eightieth birthday, and said, 'You know, I don't know what to do about this, but my driver's license has a different age on it. I know I'm going to have to take a test, but I don't want to do it this year.'

"I said, 'What's it say on the license?' He said, 'It says I'm coming up to seventy-nine.' "
—Fred Dixon, in 1985

THERE IS NO TELLING HOW FAR BACK THE ERROR ON HIS driver's license was made, or if it was intentional, and if so for what reason. When he began to drive, it was in his father's first automobile, which Foster found he couldn't stop except by running it into a curb on Yonge Street near the family home at Yonge and Roxborough. But in researching this book, as far back as clippings and records go, the present biographer kept encountering statements by Foster about his age that didn't agree with his being born 21 November 1902, his real birthday.

When he refers to the Eaton Games of 1911, when he was nearly nine, he gives his age as "seven or eight." In *Foster Hewitt: His Own Story*, published in 1967, this passage occurs: "In 1915, when I enrolled in Upper Canada

Prep School at the ripe old age of eleven. . ." He could not have been less than twelve, nearly thirteen, at the time. When he describes in the same book his first hockey broadcast on 22 March 1923, at the age of twenty: "I was just an eighteen-year-old radio announcer who had been commanded to do a chore he neither asked for nor wanted."

And in 1981, in the Toronto *Star's Today Magazine*, under his own byline: "In 1922, when I was eighteen, the Toronto *Star* opened a radio station."

It's a conundrum. He always looked younger than he was, but men to whom that happens don't usually bow to appearances; they fight against them. Because other writers who did their homework tended to take Foster's word for his age, the error was repeated in many publications and more or less perpetuated itself. It is possible that the error occurred accidentally when he got his first driver's license and instead of correcting it, he supported it for life. But at least his eightieth birthday party, which was held at the Granite Club in 1982, was right on schedule.

By the time of his eightieth, when John Bassett made a fond, sometimes funny, and always admiring toast to the guest of honor, Foster had survived, apparently with flying colors, yet another blow to his health. Those present at the party, who included every person still alive who had been with him from the earliest days to the later ones, agreed that he was the youngest-looking eighty-year-old they had ever seen as he rose to respond to John Bassett's toast, thanked him and then:

> I think it is a popular misconception that one's wisdom increases at a ratio comparable to the increase in one's advancing years. Not so, in my experience at least. I don't hear or see as well as I used to, I'm not as quick on my feet as I used to be, and if those faculties are failing I don't see how I can expect to be any wiser than I was, say ten or twenty years ago. So I have no Churchillian phrases to throw at you today simply to prove how smart I've be-

come, especially since everything else about me has been slowing down at what is getting to be an increasingly uncomfortable rate of speed.

At eighty years of age I'm afraid there is a necessity to live somewhat in the past. Most of the good things that can happen to anyone will likely have taken place by then and most of the pleasures left to us relate in large measure to what has gone before. And I do not say that with any bitterness. I consider myself very fortunate to have as many truly wonderful memories.

He went on to mention some of the memories, not only in hockey but in mining and his early days as a boxer; then:

I'm particularly proud of the role I played in popularizing hockey—and boy, how I wish we could bring back those good old days of the Kid Line, with Clancy and all that colorful gang in all their glory. . . .

Many of you have shared the good times with me and helped in no small way to make them as rewarding as they have been. I'm very grateful to you, and cannot let this opportunity go by without thanking Joan and publicly acknowledging her thoughtfulness. It [the dinner] was a great idea and I hope you've figured out how you're going to pay for it!

Thank you all, for what has been one of the very pleasant days of my life.

Taking all that at face value, one might think Foster had pretty well divorced himself from what was happening in the NHL, or more specifically Maple Leaf Gardens.

Not so. Years after he had sold his last Gardens stock, he would pore over news reports of Gardens annual meetings. After hiring Fred Dixon, he went one better. "I want you to do me a favor," he said to Fred one day. "Buy one share of Gardens stock." Foster thus would get the annual report and any other communications that went to shareholders, but the name Foster Hewitt would not be on the Gardens shareholders list, thereby showing his continued interest. But even with the rift between him and Ballard, he often said he was happy to see the Gardens doing well on the balance sheet, if not on the ice. And even the rift with Ballard had its contradictory moments. When the Leafs celebrated their fiftieth year in the Gardens, Ballard remembered with nostalgia that long-gone happy night when Foster had been master of ceremonies at the Gardens opening, on 12 November 1931.

He called Foster and said, "How about dropping the puck for us, the night we celebrate the fifty?"

Foster was delighted to go back for his final recognition in the building he had loved. When he walked out along the red carpet for the ceremonial face-off, the crowd rose for a long standing ovation.

As to the NHL, Foster wrote a piece in 1981 that was classic in its statement of continuing love for hockey and woe at what his longtime love the NHL had become. Hockey had thrilled and entertained him since he was five years old and his father started taking him along to games. He wrote.

"From that point on it's been a passionate love affair that's lasted most of this century. It's hard to explain why it means so much to me, it's simply that hockey has always been the epitome of everything. My feelings for the game remain as strong as ever, but. . . ."

It was a big *but*. He said he was not sure that the calibre of play in the NHL was even as good as it had been in the American Hockey League back when the AHL was the last rung on the ladder to the big time. He felt the NHL had grossly expanded, had outguessed itself through expansion. The bad guesses had not only been in thinking that the United States would be a good enough breeding ground to help Canada fill twenty-one teams with players of real quality. Americans had shown little real interest in hockey, he said, citing television ratings for the final game of the previous Stanley Cup playoffs: only a 4.4 percent national rating on United States television, "negligible for a national championship." Until the United States developed an interest, NHL hockey would be mediocre.

"Although the European teams have provided a source of intelligent and artistic players, that well seems to be running fairly dry, with only a trickle of stars crossing the Atlantic each year. Unless the NHL reduces the number of teams to a maximum of fifteen, preferably twelve as I think it should (although realistically I accept that it can't), I believe that the United States will have to become the saviour of the league. Where else will the players come from?"

He decried dropping the draft age from twenty to eighteen, when in the past it was almost impossible for a junior player to make the NHL. Most rookies had been around twenty-two or twenty-three and one who became a genuine superstar, Andy Bathgate, had spent five years in the minors before he earned his NHL ticket.

"The result is that many young players are coming in before they've finished learning the skills of the game. In fact, they're being taught the finer points at your expense.... Wayne Gretzky is an obvious exception, but there are too few Gretzkys and too many 'morning glories' wearing NHL sweaters when they never would in the past.

Where the dilution of quality is most telling is in the absence of great lines. I hate looking back all the time because it's the worst sin you can commit, but just imagine having a trio of Primeau, Jackson and Conacher today; or Mosienko and the two Bentleys; Boucher and the Cooks; or Lindsay, Abel and Howe. I can't think of an outstanding line in the NHL at present. And when there is one with potential, inevitably it's broken up, a theory that for the life of me I can't understand. Team play, which regrettably seems to have been replaced by individual play, is nourished by stability and refined with familiarity. The intuitive pass, the almost magical setup, requires that special sense which constant linemates acquire for each other. I never thought I would say this, but I can't name the lines on the Toronto Maple Leafs. They just don't play together long enough any more.

He went on to criticize the lack of checking skills ("if someone pops in fifty goals I wonder how many were scored against his team because he didn't back-check"), the "farcical" playoff system that cheapens the value of playoff hockey, the schedules so long that at the end fans and players alike are relieved it's over. Then:

"By talking about what I think is wrong with hockey, I feel like a kind of sitting duck. When you've been through the rigmarole for many years and you start to mastermind, you're written off as an old-time nut, which in many cases is true, I guess, because your whole outlook changes as you get older. Perhaps you expect too much, think too much of the past. But the more I argue with myself, the more I know that hockey today cannot compare to what we once had."

The year he wrote that, not long after selling CKFH, he had suffered a bowel obstruction. This was the first major operation of his life. No details were made known at the time, but after Foster started coming back to the office, he told Fred Dixon that when he'd had his radium treatments for cancer of the prostate years earlier, his bowel had been damaged. A section of it now had been taken out. No cancer had been found during that major operation, but it wasn't long before he began having trouble with his prostate again.

There's some difference in the accounts of his state of health in the early 1980s. He made that good speech, fully in control, at his eightieth birthday party. A few months earlier he had delivered a witty and fond toast to the bride when Sylvia Hough was married. (Ted and his second wife, Jean, hosted the wedding reception in their Rosedale home.) While Fred Dixon said that Foster was in the office whenever he was in the city, and was as alert as ever, at home he was said by both his wife, Joan, and his sister, Audrey, to have become withdrawn. He didn't watch television, except for a game show or two, and seemed in decline. Audrey's support for Joan's efforts during this period was unequivocal: "Joan just did everything for that man that could be done."

But when Maple Leaf Gardens celebrated its fiftieth anniversary with a special CJCL broadcast from the Gardens foyer, Foster was there, spry and cheerful, to take part along with Clancy and many other old-timers in recollecting the first times they had set foot in the place in 1931.

It was almost exactly then that Foster had a new worry, this time about Bill. A few months earlier, CKFH had been sold, but CJCL would be carrying the games on radio. In the first game of the exhibition hockey season, Bill, then fifty-three, was calling the television play-by-play for Hamilton's CHCH-TV. Some years earlier, CHCH had begun covering all Leafs games except those on Saturday nights. Suddenly in this first game Bill became very ill and could not continue. In his entire career, back to when he graduated from being a small boy at Foster's side, he had never missed a single assignment. But he had been losing weight rapidly in previous weeks and was found to have a blood disorder. It was never fully identified, but he lost fifty pounds before the weight loss could be stopped. Then he required many months of recuperation.

"During that time," Bill said, "I had a lot of time to think of living in a way that I'd obtain the most out of life. When you don't work for a full season after being as active as I have for the past thirty-odd years, you have a lot of time to think about what you'd like to do, what you are able to do and what you should do."

When he recovered and felt well enough to return to work if he decided to, he had a long talk with Foster. Fred

Dixon was also there. All Bill's reservations about going back to hockey were aired. The Canadian Sports Network had held his job for him, as he said, "Keeping the door of the gondola open for me on a game-to-game basis," while filling in the entire 1981–82 season with Dan Kelly, Dave Hodge and finally Danny Gallivan, all veteran broadcasters (but neither of the others as experienced as Gallivan). Before making any final decision on his future, Bill wanted to hear what Foster thought. After all, there'd been a Hewitt broadcasting hockey for nearly sixty years.

Foster listened, asked questions, considered and then said, "Bill, if you want to retire now, if you've had enough, that's fine by me."

For years, Bill had lived on his farm near Sunderland, Ontario, an hour's drive northeast of Toronto. After that talk with Foster, he retired "to the things I enjoy most, my wife, my children and my farm." He and his wife were among those present at Foster's eightieth birthday party a few weeks after the Canadian Sports Network bade him an affectionate farewell.

In the year following the birthday party, Foster had the first known indication that his health was deteriorating.

He and Fred Dixon had moved the Hewittdale office by then to a building at 2 Carlton Street. Two minutes' walk in any direction would take Foster to the Gardens, where he never went anymore, or to the old CKFH studios, where he had no business anymore, or to the Westbury Hotel, where he and Fred did go for lunch every day.

They always ate the same meal: a small tossed salad, a roll and a cup of coffee. They joked about the bill. Some days it would be one price and other days another. Then they had something else to joke about. One day the waiter said that the rolls, previously not charged for, were now eighty cents.

Foster, doing his Jack Benny imitation, immediately pushed his roll toward the waiter and said, "Take it back."

It might have been a joke, but from then on they didn't have rolls.

Dixon and Foster were very close by then, spending the days and some evenings together. Sometimes Foster would look depressed and worried and when asked if he felt all right, once he said, "You know, Fred, I have a little cloud over my head that I can't get rid of. If it would go I'd be fine, but I just can't get clear of that cloud."

Other friends noticed a tremendous change in Foster at about the same time. As Ted Hough said, "All his life he'd seemed so youthful, almost unchanging from one year to the next, then suddenly he aged ten or fifteen years in what seemed like just a few months."

One day Foster and Fred Dixon were lunching at the Westbury and Foster finished his salad and coffee and then sat back and asked, "Where am I?"

Then he looked off to one side and smiled at somebody. Fred glanced that way, and nobody was there.

"Foster," he said, "just relax."

Foster knew who Fred was, but didn't know where they were.

"Just relax," Fred repeated. "When you're ready to get up I'll come and help you."

A few minutes later, with Fred holding Foster's arm, they walked back to the office. In the office Foster didn't know where he was. He didn't know his own office. Fred helped him into his chair behind the desk he had left an hour or so before, and stayed with him. After a few minutes Foster started to come around. He looked around, puzzled, and said, "God, what happened to me?"

Fred said, "I think maybe you had a little stroke, or a turn of some kind."

"I don't know what's the matter," Foster said fuzzily. "That cloud is over my head again."

But he seemed to recover. Fred said he thought Foster should go home, and Foster agreed. When they were going to the parking lot, Foster said, "I'm driving home."

Fred said he would do the driving, and to give him the keys.

"No."

When they got to the car Fred said, "Give me the keys and I'll at least open the door for you."

Foster gave him the keys, whereupon Fred went around

to the passenger side and said, "You're not driving, and I've got the keys."

Foster said, "You son of a gun!"

But he did get in on the passenger side; Fred had to lift his feet into the car.

That was in middle or late 1983. A few days later Foster was back at the office, apparently as well as he had been before that incident. They carried on their daily discussions about buying and selling Foster's investments. Some time earlier, after counseling by Dixon and Donald Hill, supported by Bill, Foster had given up his lifelong contention that if a stock was worth buying it was worth holding on to. Foster's decision then was to do quite the opposite, to broaden his horizons.

He separated his holdings, in effect, into two portfolios. One, which included his remaining Baton Broadcasting stock, by then worth about seventeen million dollars, was never to be touched during his lifetime. But the other was fairly fluid. His aim was to generate a certain amount of income out of his investments. Part of that would pay office and living expenses. The rest, after taxes, would be reinvested. They bought into bonds, treasury bills, preferred shares that Foster previously had disliked, and then into common stock. Foster and Fred Dixon, with Bill often involved in the decisions, would work out each year what the target profit would be and, dealing through two or three brokers most of the time, reached or exceeded the targets every year—quite a feat given the state of the stock market in the early 1980s.

21

THE LAST YEAR

●●●

"Joan is a kind, wonderful person. You wouldn't
believe what she did for Foster. She was a
nurse to him, a companion to him, lived with
him when he was very, very hard to live with."
—Audrey Massey, eighty-six, Foster's
sister, speaking of Foster's second wife

FOSTER WAS A VERY LUCKY MAN, ALTHOUGH PERHAPS NEAR
the end he didn't always think so. The line of song that
contends it's a long, long way from May to December isn't
just whistling Dixie. Joan was forty-three and Foster a
vigorous sixty-nine when they married. In the five or so
years after Kay died, and before he met Joan, he had taken
women out from time to time but hadn't been tempted to
marry again. Maybe he and Ted Hough were having too
much fun. Both had good incomes and, within the limits
of their work, could go anywhere they wanted. It was
rarely anywhere exotic, mainly Florida, and sometimes
Ted would go along with Foster on a hockey trip—for
instance, to California when the Leafs were playing the
old California Seals or the Los Angeles Kings. They were
the two merry widowers. As Bill said, "They had a ball,
and I don't mean that disrespectfully." They were good
drinking companions and sight-seeing companions and

Foster, although nearly twenty years older than Hough, had no trouble keeping up with whatever was on the agenda.

So the age difference when Foster and Joan met and married had very little importance. They were both game for whatever came along, the trip to Moscow, vacations at the log house in Beaverton. Wendy, her husband Barry Rowan, and their family used the nearby lakeside house, and there were frequent times when Ann and Frank Somerville and their family would visit. Bill and his family had their own summer place.

Still, some things did change with marriage. When Joan and Foster met, she had her four children at home. Stu soon entered Queen's University and Sherry left for school in Switzerland. But with Donald and Barbara still at home, Foster was back living with children in the house. Joan felt that he wasn't as comfortable with them as he once might have been, but it wasn't a major problem. Foster's prostate trouble and treatments, even when that crisis passed, slowed him up a little but the telling change in his energy level, as compared to Joan's, was yet to come.

Eventually, as the 1970s wore on into the 1980s, the alteration in their relationship was more a reflection of Foster's age and the beginning of uncertain health than anything else. Joan undoubtedly noticed his decline sooner than anyone. When he was at his office, she had other things to do, many friends, trips that she took herself or, once, a Florida vacation with Audrey. They had become friends as soon as they met, at a time when Foster had been taking Joan out a lot and Audrey said, "You'd better bring her over so we can have a look at this person you're so interested in." Audrey was to be a stalwart friend. As Joan said later, "I had her shoulder to cry on."

Foster, more and more, once he got home from the office, wasn't inclined to stir out again except for the occasional dinner and certain major occasions, one of these being the eightieth birthday party that Joan had done much to arrange.

Joan rejects the idea that after that occasion Foster began to show symptoms of Alzheimer's disease, a degenerative brain disorder that for many years was often thought, wrongly, to be senility. The disease was first diagnosed in 1906 by the German neurologist, Alois Alzheimer, but has only recently become common in medical language. One thing agreed on by researchers is that there is, at least at present, no prevention and no cure.

According to Foster's doctors, he had Alzheimer's for almost the last two years of his life, but probably was only in the first stage of the disease. This stage is characterized by forgetfulness and other behavior sometimes found in an overworked brain. No evidence is available that he ever reached the second stage, often manifested by increasing paranoia and aggressive outbursts that tend to alienate other family members and friends. So Joan has some reason to believe that Foster's problems were simply due to normal processes of aging, plus the after effects of his bowel operation.

"I think that was the beginning of the end," she said later. "They had him on morphine and other drugs. He was a long time coming out of the anesthetic and afterwards he didn't even remember having the operation."

Early in 1984 he and Joan went to Florida. After their return in the spring, she felt he was declining rapidly. To try to interest him, she sometimes would throw a party, but Foster tended just to sit in a corner and not take part. He had passed the test for his driver's license, but did not drive any more. Joan would drive him to the office when he wished, "and when he got tired he would phone and I would go and drive him home."

Although his friends did notice that he had aged rapidly in appearance, Joan was closer to what was happening.

"We have to face it, he was getting older and sitting around here for most of a year, his mind wasn't doing anything, he wouldn't even read the paper. He watched some television but wasn't taking it in. He wouldn't even watch hockey, because he said it was so awful—and I think it reminded him, too, of better times."

She said that he often spoke rather despairingly about the way he felt. By late in 1984 he complained often that something was wrong with him, and that the doctors weren't doing the right things.

Joan recalls:

> It just sort of went from bad to worse. He'd say, "I just have to get back into the hospital. I want to get cured, I want to be better, I hate this." I'd phone the doctor and he'd drop in to see him and take his blood pressure and say everything is coming along fine and put him on another pill. He was taking a lot of pills. He had a rash. I don't know whether it had to do with the pills he was taking, but they'd try something else and make him feel horrible in some other way.
>
> Finally just before Christmas he said again, "I just want to go to the hospital and get better." So on Boxing Day he went into Wellesley Hospital. They told me they could only keep him in a private room for a couple of weeks, then I'd have to find something else. The Providence Villa [an eight-hundred-bed hospital with chronic-care facilities owned by the Sisters of Saint Joseph] seemed the answer, but it is very difficult to get into. I called Doug Bassett at CFTO. I understood later that all kinds of influence had to be brought to bear, but with the help of Ted Delaney, a vice-president at CFTO, we got him in there.

Ted Delaney is chairman of the board at Providence Villa. "We had a waiting list of nearly a thousand," he said later. "But I went to the Sisters and said we just had to find room for Foster Hewitt. Which they did."

Foster's last few months seemed to have been without worry or pain. His family and friends visited often. Ted Hough's experience seems to have been typical.

"I checked carefully ahead of time with Fred Dixon," this old friend of hundreds of happy times said, adding:

Fred was the one who was closest to him in the last couple of years in terms of sharing things. I wanted to know if it would be appropriate for me to go and see him.

Fred said, "Yes, he'd love to see you and love to see a lot of other people, too, that had dropped from his life. But don't be upset if he doesn't recognize you or if he lives in the past."

So I went out there and went up to the fourth floor and turned to go down to his room. I'm reluctant to go to hospitals and funeral parlors, places like that; they bother me, and I didn't know what to expect. But suddenly there's Foster being wheeled down the aisle by a nurse and from fifty feet away he lifted his hand to wave and call, 'Hi, Ted!' The same cheery greeting I would have gotten at any time, and that just set the tone for a two-hour visit with him.

The nurse had been taking him to the dining room. She said, "Mr. Hewitt, you want to visit with your friend, so . . ."

"No," Foster said, "I'll have my meal and he can sit in my room and wait for me and I'll come back." But the nurse said she would bring Foster's meal to his room and we could sit there and chat while he ate.

And that's what we did, but his mind soon turned back. All the hockey trips we'd made together, hotel rooms we'd sat in and had a few drinks and talked, his mind had made a shift and we were living a hockey trip in Boston. He'd look at his watch, or where his watch should be, and say, "Well, it's time to go to the game now, Ted." We were getting ready to go to the game. "Where are we going to eat after

209

the game?" he said. And we were planning where we'd go to eat after the game. I went along with it. It was fun. It can't be so bad, that kind of thing, when even if your mind does change gears it's back to a time when you were happy and involved and having fun.

On another visit Foster's lane change took them in a different direction.

I used to visit him often up in Beaverton, you know. In winter he loved to go snowmobiling, he had a couple of Skidoos, and we'd go out on the Lake Simcoe ice and roar around. He had the lake house and the log cabin across the road but in fact he liked the log cabin, used to barbecue there in a big stone pit that he had built himself at the back. We talked about that as if it was right now. He would always cook with wood and get a blazing fire going. We'd have to have several drinks while he waited for the white ash to be just right.

A trick of his in barbecuing was to take a green cedar bough and throw it into the fire just as he was finishing the steak and let it smoke; no barbecuing was complete without the cedar for the last three or four minutes, smoking the meat. We'd done that many times.

Well, this time he knew he was in the hospital, but told me he was leaving to drive to Beaverton. "Would you and Jean like to come up?" I said sure, so he said, "Fine, I'll be downstairs in an hour and you can pick me up and we'll drive up together."

This was on a Friday and I said, "Well, no, I've got to go back to work this afternoon, you go up on your own and I'll drive up Sunday morning with Jean and we'll spend the day with you."

"Okay," he said, and got up and looked out of the window and said, "Weather doesn't look very good, does it? It's going to rain. But we'll have a barbecue anyway."

The time changes in Foster's mind often took him back to the 1960s or earlier. Sometimes he mentioned his first wife, Kay, as if she were still alive. He did not always recognize people who came to see him. Joan's visits were frequently difficult when she would find herself involved with situations she had never known. Wendy, visiting once after she had been very ill herself, said that Foster seemed withdrawn that day, lost in thoughts of his own.

But the people he had been closest to he usually recognized immediately before he drifted into the past. Fred Dixon was one of them, except that Foster always assumed Fred had been with him all his life, instead of ten years or so.

Fred: "I went in to see Foster once and he said, 'Hi, Fred. How are things in Peterborough?' I didn't know what he meant but I said, 'Oh, they're fine,' and he said, 'I'm glad to hear it.' A little later I was talking to Ted Hough and told him about that and asked if he could shed any light on what was supposed to be happening in Peterborough. 'I sure can,' he said. 'The Leafs used to have their training camp there. Next time ask him about the Empress Hotel.' So the next time Foster brought up Peterborough it was something about going there. I said, 'Where are you going to stay, at the Empress?'

" 'Oh, yes,' Foster said. 'That's where I always stay.' "

Near the end, when his faculties were failing rapidly, his condition was complicated by kidney failure. On a Friday late in April, with Bill and Wendy there, he wasn't able to speak. The end was near, but Bill felt that when he talked, asked a couple of little questions, his father heard.

"His eyes told me that he had heard, there's a language of the eyes, even without words."

211

For the next two days, he was often unconscious. On Sunday afternoon Joan visited and sat with him awhile. "He recognized me," she said, "but couldn't speak."

A little before 5 P.M. on that day, 21 April 1985, she left to have dinner with Audrey. Soon after she arrived, a nurse called and said Joan should come quickly, that Foster was failing rapidly. Five minutes later, as Joan was hurrying out, the nurse called again and said he had died.

The voice that had been the best-known in Canada was silenced forever. Headlines across the country the next day told the story:

His Voice Is Silenced but the Memory Lingers
Leaf Broadcaster a True Superstar
Death of a Legend

INDEX

213

215

216